Write
to the
Point

*How to Communicate in Business With
Style and Purpose*

By

Salvatore J. Iacone, Ph.D.

CASTLE BOOK**S**

This edition published in 2005 by
CASTLE BOOKS ®
A division of Book Sales, Inc.

114 Northfield Avenue
Edison, NJ 08837

This edition published by arrangement with
Career Press
3 Tice Road
Franklin Lakes, NJ 07417

Write to the Point © 2003 by Salvatore J. Iacone.
Edited by JODI BRANDON
Typeset by JOHN J. O'SULLIVAN
Original English language edition published by Career Press

Iacone, Salvatore, J.
Write to the point : how to communicate in business with style and purpose / by
Salvatore J. Iacone.
p. cm.
    Includes index.
    1.   Business writing—Handbooks, manuals, etc. 2. Business
       communication—Handbooks, manuals, etc. 3. English
       language—Business English. I. Title.

HF5718.3 .I236 2003
808'.06665—dc21   2002031568

ISBN-13: 978-0-7858-2093-2
ISBN-10: 0-7858-2093-0

Printed in the United States of America

Dedication

To Martha Grace

...ever under the Moon and planet Venus

Acknowledgments

There are a number of people whose help I very much appreciated in writing this book. To begin, my agent, Susan Ann Protter, for suggesting I submit the initial proposal to Michael Lewis, Senior Acquisitions Editor at Career Press. Thanks to Mike for his support and confidence in getting the book accepted. Next, the inimitable Jane Jensen, for her diligent, skillful review and editorial suggestions regarding the first draft.

I also want to thank Jackie Michaels, Publicity Director; Kirsten Beucler, Marketing Coordinator; Stacey Farkas, Editorial Director; John J. O'Sullivan, Associate Editorial Director; Jodi Brandon, my copy editor; and all production and sales staff at Career Press.

To my mother, Stella, and to my children Alexis, Hadley, and Evan, my infinite thanks for their enduring love and encouragement.

Contents

Introduction

What Is This Book About?

WRITE TO THE POINT IS an informal step-by-step guide to improving the writing skills of business and technical professionals for both traditional and modern electronic forms of written communication. The goal of this guide to better business writing is to help you to write with greater ease, precision, and clarity. A conversational instructional format will "walk" you through the actual stages of the writing process, from planning and writing the first draft to editing and proofreading. Also included are helpful guidelines to correct grammar, punctuation, and modern usage; lists of often-confused words; and models of suggested content and formats for e-mail, memos, letters, and reports.

Who Will Find This Book Useful?

All levels of business and technical personnel whose writing skills are essential to job performance and productivity will find this easy-to-read guide to better written communication invaluable and immediately useful for their daily needs. Upper-level and middle managers and supervisors who need to provide guidance to their staffs, administrative assistants whose duties include editing and proofreading letters and memos, and technical support professionals who prepare instructions, procedures and documentation will find this book helpful to written communication. *Write to the Point* will also benefit the general writer, those for whom English is a second language, and students preparing to write college entry essays. My hope is for *Write to the Point* to be welcome by all writers.

What Is the Focus of This Book?

Successful business writing is responsive, well organized, clear to the reader, and appropriate in tone. *Write to the Point* is designed to share with you proven techniques for writing for business with greater clarity and precision and less stress. This book consists of 12 chapters organized to reflect the actual stages of the writing process: planning, organizing, writing, editing, and proofreading. Several chapters include examples and models of various types of business correspondence, such as memos, letters, and reports suitable for immediate practical application. One chapter is devoted exclusively to writing successful e-mail. Throughout the book, many helpful lists of words and phrases are included. The various appendices focus on reviewing basic principles of grammar, punctuation, and usage to ensure mechanical correctness.

How Is This Book Different From Other Business Writing Books?

Write to the Point (1) provides guidelines for achieving greater precision that will also lessen the stress business professionals experience when writing under the increased demands on their time due to e-mail, voice mail, meetings, and so on; (2) offers solutions to realistic rather than theoretical writing problems; (3) presents techniques for improving the effectiveness and clarity of e-mail as well as traditional correspondence; (4) employs an analytical approach to improving both content and structure; (5) incorporates actual realistic models to support "step-by-step" instruction to writing successful e-mail, memos, and letters; and (6) includes appendices that review basic principles of standard English grammar, punctuation, and usage.

1

Writing to the Point

*"The difficulty is not to write,
but to write what you mean."*
—Robert Louis Stevenson

WRITING IN BUSINESS HAS NEVER been more difficult and more stressful. We live in an age of information overload thanks to e-mail, voice mail, cell phones, and pagers. Although all these wonders were designed to make life and communication easier and faster, they have also created added demands on our time. Writers are expected to respond quickly to an endless flow of e-mail messages. What results is that readers complain about an increasing lack of clarity and abundance of mechanical errors. Supervisors and managers express bewilderment at employees' inability to simply state the essence of what they need to express or neglect to apply appropriate tone and sense of decorum. The best and brightest of technical professionals have difficulty communicating clearly with their peers and non-technical readers whose software glitches, system problems, and changes they must address daily. They often experience frustration whenever writing to readers with little or limited understanding of their technical expertise. The challenge for technical writers is how to bridge that gap when writing for readers with limited technical expertise. It's no wonder an "information gap" frequently exists between technical and non-technical readers given the rapid daily changes in information technology.

In every writing seminar I have taught, people complain about how every day more and more time is devoted to responding to e-mail and voice mail, to say nothing of the daily demands of generating traditional correspondence (such as reports and letters) and attending meetings. Still others believe the increasing pressure to respond immediately to e-mail results in their writing or receiving fragmented, confusing messages that are either too long or short or too technical.

Perhaps one training manager expressed it best when he told me that all he hoped for after sending someone to a writing seminar was simply that he be able to understand what the writer was trying to tell him. He wondered if that was asking for too much. Of course not, I answered. After all, what is the point of writing if not to express our thoughts clearly to our readers? Isn't that what writing is all about? Of course, but sadly enough, writing to the point is often easier said than done for most of us.

All of the above advice is easy to say and sounds fine in theory, but how do you apply this to real life? Writing is usually never easy and almost always a challenge and stressful. So maybe the first step to better business writing is to try to eliminate the stress.

Writing Without Stress: Is It Possible?

No writer has ever really written without stress, so how can I promise to help you achieve such a state? After all, even masterful writers from Homer to Shakespeare to Stephen King would hardly concede that writing is easy. Psychologists often tell us that to relieve stress we either have to remove the reason or stimulus, learn to accept it, or transform it from a negative experience into a positive one. So simply trying to create the first sentence is cause enough for writers to experience stress, and no wonder, because when writing we almost have to become godlike: We must create something from nothing.

Then there is another reason we experience stress when attempting to write. No matter how logical or commonsensical we all like to believe we are, when it comes to the writing process we all struggle with the need to impose order on the chaos of ideas and impressions our minds are seeking to express. If writing can be defined as "thinking on paper" (or, nowadays, in cyberspace), doing so with ease and precision has become ever more difficult. Why? Technology, for one reason. Just think about how many times during a routine business day we face the temptations of hitting that good old "send" key to move on to our next message or to respond to the seemingly impatient inquiries of those sending us e-mail messages. Everyone seems in a hurry these days. So many incoming e-mail messages have a sense of urgency to them that we begin to wonder what is *not* urgent! Instantaneous response has become the watchword of written electronic communication. Why wait for a well-written response tomorrow when you can get a poorly written one today?

There are also emotional, physical, and mental obstacles to getting started and moving beyond the blank page or computer monitor. Perhaps we're too tired, worried about an ailing child at home, coming down with a cold, or just don't feel like writing for whatever reason. After all, we're people, not machines. Inspiration, that mysterious mechanism that generates ideas, is not a lightbulb we can turn on or off at will.

As for perfection, forget it. If you could speak with the greatest writers about their masterpieces, they would all no doubt admit: "I could have made it better." Perhaps Shakespeare's Hamlet could have been funnier or Melville's Captain Ahab a bit less obsessed with that elusive white whale.

Another source of stress is the equation of quantity versus quality. I cannot imagine anyone arriving to work on a Monday morning to find a 500-page report on his or her desk and saying "I can't wait to read this." The poet Robert Browning wrote that "less is more." In most daily business writing, that idea will often prove that this rule applies. At the same time, writing less for its own sake is not the solution if we leave out important details or information or create a choppy, fragmented sentence pattern. Rather, given the demands of modern business life, we have to ask ourselves this simple question: Would I want to read my own writing? How would I react to my e-mail message or trip report? Would I delete the e-mail or wish the report included a summary because I haven't the time, need, interest, or desire to read the entire document? The ancient wisdom of placing ourselves in the reader's shoes works perfectly well here.

An additional source of stress is trying to figure out how best to express our thoughts to our various readers, whether they be coworkers anywhere in the world. Who are these people and how do we best succeed in communicating with them without ambiguity or confusion? What's the best way to ask a delicate question? Which words would serve best? Ask yourself: Are my writing skills reflecting in a positive light my educational and professional background, knowledge, and understanding of the topic at hand?

Above all, the very demands of the writing process create stress for us. Which words will best do here? How about the organization of details? Is my central message clear or did I bury it somewhere on page 3? Should I use sentences or lists or illustrations? Have I revised and polished the writing to a brilliant shimmer or dulled it out of existence? Are there mistakes in grammar, punctuation, spelling, or usage that will tarnish my professional image? How about the tone? Is it appropriate or have I stepped over that line of over-familiarity or rude innuendo? Will my boss approve the memo or will I suffer the traumatic rejection highlighted in red ink?

We end up asking more questions than Hamlet and, in so doing, can easily become as disinclined to translating our thoughts into actions.

Good writing requires time and discipline. The sole temptation often most difficult for us to resist is, to paraphrase Oscar Wilde, the temptation to race through the writing as soon as possible so we can move on to the next task. Yet when we give in to this temptation, we find time and again that the old adage rings true: Haste indeed makes waste, or at least requires rewriting. Yet because writing expresses thinking, whether on paper or in cyberspace, we need to find an approach to transforming what is abstract and invisible (our thoughts) into a tangible, visible, concrete form of communication.

When in Doubt, Write Nothing

English novelist George Eliot once observed: "Blessed is the man who, having nothing to say, abstains from giving in words evidence of the fact."

In daily life, sometimes the best response is no response, whether to a sarcastic remark or hostile gesture. So too is it on occasion that the best choice is to refrain from putting in writing your thoughts, ideas, complaints, suggestions, advice, or any other information you may need to communicate. Doing nothing is sometimes the right thing to do. Doing nothing is in itself a decision. So even though all writing consists of three major stages (planning, writing, and editing), you may want to consider another stage: preplanning, the decisive moment during which you need to seriously question if you should write at all.

For instance, let's assume an otherwise competent associate has botched an important potential deal or seemingly simple task. Your first inclination might be to fire off an angry, disappointed, and/or frustrated-sounding memo or e-mail chastising the poor devil for his or her failings. On second thought, you worry that if the senior vice president somehow sees a copy, your coworker's job performance may be called into serious question, or worse. You wouldn't want that, so instead of writing you decide a private discussion would suit you just as well. The poor soul will still be able to perceive your feelings from your tone of voice and facial expressions. Moreover, the strong disappointment you feel will be expressed, but so too will your understanding that occasionally things go wrong for the best of us, you included. Nothing personal, you might say, only a friendly little chat that allows you to convey your point but allows the listener to know you don't hate him or her.

Questioning the need for any writing you plan to do is a primary worthwhile consideration that can save you and your reader time and effort. Whether the message consists of your observations prior to a meeting or a suggestion that a report might best be conveyed through an audio-visual rather than written presentation, always consider alternatives to writing that may prove far more effective and appropriate.

The First Step: Relax, It's Only Writing

Some people work very well under pressure. Others tend to become frazzled and overwhelmed. Most of us are perhaps a combination of both tendencies. To lessen the anxiety and tension inherent in the writing process, we need to try to relax a bit. We need to understand the important roles relaxation and diversion play in helping us unlock and release our thoughts and help us avoid unnecessary frustration and anxiety.

Don't feel that you have to write immediately. Get a cup of coffee or tea, make some phone calls, chat with the person across the room about last night's baseball game, do some knee bends or other stretching exercises, maybe even go for a walk during lunchtime. Do anything but write. Very often, while we are engaged in other activities, ideas begin to emerge unexpectedly. As thoughts occur to you, whether in the form of words, impressions, phrases, or questions, jot them down on a notepad. We can't make inspiration happen by willpower alone. Nor is there any magic potion or pill to take to release that mechanism we call inspiration. As Shakespeare might have phrased it: "Would it were so."

Next: Pay Attention to Your Environment

Travelers to unfamiliar destinations are often advised to be aware of their surroundings to avoid encountering unpleasant situations, such as being mugged. Environment can affect our ability to concentrate. Trying to write in an office where there is constant noise or next to an open window where traffic passes ceaselessly is not an ideal environment. Ironically, dead silence can often be the loudest distraction of all. Some of us thrive amidst chaos and activity. Others need the privacy and quiet offered by an empty conference room, library, or unoccupied office. Still others get their best ideas on a train or bus or driving to work. You need to do a little self-analysis regarding where and how you write best.

The trick to establishing the environment most conducive for you to write is to find a place that feels most comfortable. You might work best in an unoccupied conference room, a quiet cafeteria between breakfast and lunch hours, or even that enduring citadel of original thoughts: the restroom. Perhaps sitting at your own desk is the best place to start. You're on familiar ground. Of course, one problem is that people know where to find you. You can be interrupted by phone calls or instant e-mail messages and the usual round of unexpected work-related problems. Still, it's home, and that is often where the heart is.

Piano Lessons Alone Will Not Make You Mozart

One of the greatest literary figures of the 18th century, Samuel Johnson, observed that "what is written without effort is read without pleasure." Wise words indeed. Johnson knew that good writing could only result from hard work and discipline. In fact, perhaps Johnson would agree that even when the writing appears to be going well, it still *ain't* easy, folks.

The truth is that some people just have a rare, natural talent for effortlessly putting their ideas down on paper logically, precisely, and economically. Most of us have to struggle with making sense and then imposing order on the chaos in our heads, all those impressions, feelings, and ideas. I have always advised those who attend my writing seminars that you can take piano lessons, but that won't make you Mozart, and painting lessons alone will not

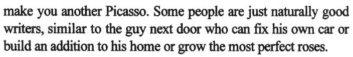

make you another Picasso. Some people are just naturally good writers, similar to the guy next door who can fix his own car or build an addition to his home or grow the most perfect roses.

Writing is a skill and thus can be learned, but natural ability is something else. Very few people can sit down and clearly relate their thoughts at the first attempt. This is true for professional writers as well, whether novelists or journalists, because the writing process involves three inescapable elements: planning, actual writing, and editing. All writing requires more than one draft if it is to be any good. Only by reviewing and revising can we transform rough ideas into shimmering jewels of expression. All diamonds require polishing, and so do our thoughts.

Accepting the need to revise our work enables us to feel less hurried and perhaps more patient and disciplined in approaching writing assignments. We need to develop a realistic attitude toward the demands of transforming jumbled masses of data, observations, notes, and ideas into a cohesive reader-friendly document. Otherwise, we may experience "information overload," a feeling of being overwhelmed, trapped, or swamped simply by the sheer amount of information we need to convey. Ultimately, outlines, lists, summaries, and any other structural elements of writing can help us organize and impose a structure on the material. At the same time, we must first struggle our way out of a quagmire of doubt, frustration, and indecision that can lead to the nemesis of all writers: procrastination.

So where do we begin? Where else but with ourselves, alone and armed with little more than our thoughts and the need to express them?

2

Getting Started: Stop Staring and Start Writing

"My way is to begin at the beginning."
—Lord Byron

"The last thing one knows when writing a book is what to put first."
—Blaise Pascal

IF ONLY WRITING WERE LIKE riding a bike, swimming, driving a car, or roller-skating. Once learned, we never forget how to do it. Unlike climbing a mountain and planting a flag on its peak, the writing process consists of mental mountain climbing where there is no peak to reach. Rather, we encounter only a series of plateaus of elevation. Two factors often inhibit the writing process: fear of criticism or failure and the need to impress the reader. Our awareness or sense of permanence associated with committing ideas to paper or the computer disk can produce in us feelings of anxiety and lead to procrastination. We are often reluctant to reveal our thinking on paper because any resulting criticism either from superiors or readers will reflect negatively on our ability to think clearly and logically. We are what we write, or perhaps what we seem.

Often only through our writing do others know us. So it is natural for us to become concerned about the image we convey. In a way, as writers we are similar to movie stars who wince at the thought of an inferior performance or ill-chosen role captured forever on film. We too can easily dread that what we write today may haunt us tomorrow. If the actor or performer who claims he or she never reads reviews cannot be believed, business writers who try to convince themselves that they write only for themselves, the reader be damned, are not to be trusted as well. With the exception of what we record in a diary, writing is meant to be shared with readers. Writing is a dialogue with our readers, not a monologue.

Since the days of our earliest English classes, we writers have been especially prone to the tyranny of the red pen. It is not surprising that we can become traumatized, so to speak, about exposing our thoughts to the public reader. No one enjoys being criticized negatively. If fear can paralyze the bravest soldier, it is no wonder that the freedom of expression and spontaneity essential to effective writing is vulnerable to being stifled from within. The greatest writers from Shakespeare to Dickens to those of our own time have often shown us the strongest prisons are those without walls and steel bars and doors, they are the mental and emotional interior ones we create for ourselves.

Express to Impress

What kind of writing makes the best impression? Writing that is readable. Writing that conveys your ideas with clarity and precision. Writing that allows your reader to conclude, *I understand every word this person is trying to express.* We are in big trouble if our readers ask, *Is this what you really wanted to or were trying to say? Did I misinterpret your meaning here?*

We are not writing interpretive poetry, where the reader may think we are saying this or that. Business writing does not involve mystery or the need for interpretation. Worse, writing is often an all-or-nothing proposition. We are not there to explain our message to the reader. We are not available to say, "This is what I really wanted to say" or "Let me put it another way" or "Let me draw you a diagram." No. It's an all-or-nothing proposition.

So then what type of writing makes the best impression? There is only one: writing that communicates our thoughts clearly and precisely. Too many writers get caught up in the notion that the only acceptable models for writing appear in formal reports, newspapers, magazines, trade or professional journals, and, heaven protect us, academic articles. Do you really want to send an e-mail or letter in overly verbose academic or formal style? Although both styles have their places, for the most part, they will most likely put your busy business reader to sleep. Fancy words and long-winded sentences do not make for successful writing. Rather, it's the skillful way we use words as tools to create and connect sentences.

It's Time to Jump Into the Water

One way to overcome our initial resistance or fear of writing is to accept the fact that there is no such thing as perfect writing, at least not in this world. Even if it should exist, there would be critics to find fault with it. Yet this does not mean we should assume a devil-may-care attitude or ignore the needs of the reader. Rather, we need, for the moment, to disregard all concerns of criticism and desires to impress and just start writing. In the same manner that the longer a 10-year-old first learning to swim waits to overcome the hesitation to jump into the deep end of the pool, we as writers must "dive" into the pool of ideas we want to express. No one ever learns to ski without sooner or later going down the mountain. You can't learn to sky dive without leaving the plane. Unlike the just-described experiences, there is no way to simulate the writing process. We are always jumping out of a real plane, albeit a mental one, when scribbling our first draft. No wonder we hesitate.

Face the Blank Page: Overcoming Writer's Block

All writers experience writer's block, the inability to begin or continue to develop ideas. Because we are people and not machines, it is only natural that the road to written communication is fraught with unforeseen detours and potholes. Any number of reasons can lead to this frustrating experience. We might be worried about a personal or job-related problem, fearful of criticism from our supervisors, or just plain too exhausted or not in the mood to write even the shortest of sentences. So what can we do about this frustrating dilemma? Sometimes doing nothing is the best course of action. We might concentrate on another activity.

Perhaps we may decide it best to tend to other matters. All of these techniques buy us time to get back to writing. When you experience writer's block, here are a number of techniques that will help relieve your stress and perhaps to find direction.

Revisit the Past

Use your previous writing as a model. Thanks to our computers, we can save all our correspondence, good and bad, for later review. So if you find that your writing assignment is similar to one accomplished previously, such as a memo, letter to a customer, report, or manual, there's little harm in using it as a point of departure. Surely this solution is better than the ceaseless torment of staring at the page or blank monitor. If the content and format of your model worked before, it may well work again. Yet there is a negative aspect of this technique: Just as it's not always a good idea to dwell too much on the past, the tendency to rely too heavily on previous writing may inhibit your chances for growing as a writer and may produce feelings of boredom both for you and your reader.

Go Idea Shopping

You don't always have to begin writing complete sentences. A "shopping" list of ideas, problems, and topics we need to address will often do just fine. There's something about a list that helps us to focus our thoughts. Once listed, you can expand upon the word or phrase you jotted down. Perhaps you might even number each in order of importance. You can add or delete topics. Most importantly, you've begun writing.

Use a Conversational Style

Some people are better talkers than they are writers. They have the ability to tell us in the clearest terms what we need to know. Yet when they send us e-mail or letters, we wonder why a Dr. Jekyll of spoken clarity and precision has been transformed into a Mr. Hyde of written obscurity and verboseness. E-mail alone has encouraged greater use of conversational style in writing, and to a great extent that's good. Unfortunately, some writers mistakenly believe a conversational style gives them license to write incomprehensible fragment and run-on sentences or cross the line of decorum.

The great advantage of conversational writing is the ability to generate words and phrases most appropriate to spoken language, often reflective of the informal, lively rhythms of our speech. When we speak, we use voice inflections, gestures, facial expressions, and body language. Our writing relies more heavily on complete sentences, precise words, and an orderly presentation of ideas. So if you're a better talker than writer, why not write initially the way you would say it to someone face-to-face, during a phone conference, or in a meeting? You can always modify your conversational notes to sound more like writing. That is, instead of the vague "get back to me," you would substitute a specific action word such as *call, meet,* or *advise.* Again, you've begun the writing process.

Engage in Free-Writing

I often think of this technique as a mental laxative or a "when all else fails" antidote for writer's block. First, set a time limit, say five to 20 minutes. Next, identify your subject, purpose, and reader. Then begin writing anything and everything that may come to mind about the identified subject, purpose, and/or reader. Describe your feelings or fears or concerns or expectations. Focus on what you want to say or what the reader needs to do. You might even use first sentences such as "I don't know what I want to say about..." or "What I really need to say here is..." or even "I don't feel like writing this message because..." as motivating opening lines. **Do not stop** to edit. Just write.

The idea behind this technique is to attempt to trigger the ever-elusive inspiration through perspiration. So don't worry about generating an orderly list of sentences or if you write the conclusion before providing the supporting details or an opening sentence. Just keep going, much as you would after your car battery has died and someone has helped you jump-start the engine. You keep driving until you get to the nearest service station or home.

When your writing time expires, take out your own red pen and review your work. It's time to engage in intellectual "cutting and pasting." What's worth keeping? What needs to be deleted? Look for meaningful phrases and sentences, important details, examples, or recommendations—in short, anything that would be useful to expressing your message. Try to rearrange ideas in order of importance and relevance. List and number instructions or procedures. Remember also that when getting started on your first draft and during the transition from thinking to actual writing, it is best to get your ideas down quickly without concern for correct grammar, punctuation, usage, and spelling.

Most importantly, remember that although this is not a first draft, rather a beginning of the beginning, at least you're no longer staring at the page or monitor. In fact, you've taken a giant step, however uncertain, toward creating a first draft.

3

It's Not About You:
Writing for Your Reader

"If the writer doesn't sweat, the reader will."
—Mark Twain

IF YOU WALK INTO A store looking for a new computer and the first salesperson you meet immediately points to a group of computers and says, "Any of those are good," and then walks away, there is a good chance so will you, and with good reason. Why? You were never asked what you were seeking, how much you could spend, or if the computer would be used for business or pleasure or your child's homework assignments. In brief, the salesperson never considered or asked about your needs and preferences. Just as it would come as no surprise to learn the salesperson who was indifferent to a potential customer's needs was soon out of a job, the same holds true for writers who ignore their readers. The reader is the writer's "customer" and one whose business or approval is one we need to seek. The more you know about your reader, the greater the chances you will meet his or her needs and expectations.

Would you want to receive any of these examples of poor business writing?

No-Sympathy Letter

Dear Mr. Lowry:

   We are sorry for any discomfort you may have experienced in attempting to use our suppository product, but we can't assume any blame for your failing to carefully read the directions. How in heaven's name could you have imagined that you did not have to remove the foil before use?

Huh? Letter

Dear Ms. Francis:

   I am writing in response to a letter addressed to me from Victor Heflin, who is employed by your company. We briefly discussed this letter on the telephone today. All parties will be copied for edification. Initially by copy of this letter we wish to convey our apology as a company for an infraction of your company policy committed by one of our sales reps and that ultimately became confrontational. We wish to respond to let you know that our company takes such matters seriously. Pilferage of goods by our people is nefarious behavior and thus a serious event. What has transpired is done and it will serve no purpose to revisit this event.

   Going forward, then, we want you to be assured that the transgressing individual has been reprimanded and advised that further infractions of this nature will not be tolerated. Next time he's out the door, in plain English.

Headache-Causing Insurance Procedures

   You are not insured for any risk which you incur in providing directly or through your subcontractors if such risk also arises from a service provided by you which is stated in your policy of insurance to be a service for which you are not insured.

"I Love to Hear Myself Talk" Memo

In reviewing bid comparisons for computer equipment consideration should be given to the selection of equipment which duplicates that already in service and that is already providing good performance. Sometimes selection of computer equipment is accomplished with small price difference between the lowest price and the price for equipment already installed in our office. In such an instance as this, careful consideration of such comparative buying should include the economics of purchasing and learning to use entirely different hardware or software as compared to purchasing computers duplicate to the ones already installed and in use in our department. Therefore, it is believed advantageous that full consideration of the initial cost of new computer equipment and software is sufficient justification in most instances for the selection of such equipment which would duplicate existing equipment.

✎ ✎ ✎

Wouldn't you prefer to receive these "reader-friendly" messages?

Good Letter #1

Dear Ms. Olsen:

As requested in your letter of July 5, enclosed is a copy of our annual report for your review. We very much appreciate your interest in our company and hope you find the information suitable to your needs.

Sincerely,
Stella Stahr

Good Letter #2

Dear Mr. Mature:

Thank you for writing regarding your unfortunate accident. We sincerely are relieved to learn you did not seriously injure yourself in attempting to repair your roof.

At the same time, please note that our "Home Repair Guide for the Intellectually Challenged" emphatically advises anyone preparing to perform roof repairs to first secure a rope around his or her waist and anchor it to a stationary object such as a nearby tree, chimney, or other permanent structure.

Nowhere does our manual ever suggest that you tie the rope from your waist to the handle, bumper, or any other part of any vehicle parked directly below. Although it is most unfortunate that your wife did not see the rope leading from your car up to the roof before she backed out of your driveway, we can assume no legal responsibility for the injuries you incurred.

Sincerely,

Frank Christopher

Customer Service

Ask Before You Write

Your job is easier when writing for someone you know either at work or in another company. Maybe you've exchanged e-mail messages, spoken routinely by phone, or even met for lunch. As a result, you are likely to be familiar with the reader's expectations, technical skills or limitations, appreciation of visual aids, and preference for substantial or minimum amount of details.

Frequently, when writing to customers, vendors, and representatives of large organizations or government agencies, you will have little or no knowledge of the reader's background and needs. Of course, no writer can be expected to be a mind reader or be expected to review a reader's resume before setting pen to paper. Yet there are a number of questions to ask before writing a word, such as the following:

What Do I Know About My Reader?

Are you writing for someone within your department or company? If so, then you may be familiar with what this reader already knows or needs to know about your subject. If you are writing upwards to your supervisor, you may well be familiar with style and format preferences. He or she may love lists or hate them, prefer familiar words or be impressed by fancier ones, or appreciate shorter paragraphs. Perhaps your best approach is to write in an informal conversational style that includes contractions and personal pronouns.

If you're writing to or for someone outside your organization you have neither met nor previously sent correspondence, avoid using acronyms or abbreviations to prevent confusion or misinterpretation. Your style may be formal but not stuffy or too impersonal. Don't pontificate.The general tone should be businesslike (cordial but serious). Take more time to review and edit and proofread your message because its quality, or lack of it, represents not just you but your organization.

What Are His or Her Needs or Expectations?

When you respond to an incoming e-mail or letter you have the benefit of having a reasonably clear understanding of your reader's needs or expectations. You know your goal is either to provide information, meet a request, respond to a question or complaint, suggest a solution, or offer instructions and guidance. Remember to always address the reader's concerns before expressing any of yours. It's not about you.

When initiating correspondence, think of your reader as the customer. Then imagine yourself in the reader's position. How would you want someone to respond to your problem or clarify an issue you found confusing? What type of opening sentence or message would attract and hold your attention? If

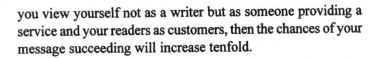

you view yourself not as a writer but as someone providing a service and your readers as customers, then the chances of your message succeeding will increase tenfold.

Is the Subject Matter of Great or Little Interest?

When you are reasonably certain your reader will find your subject of interest, your job is an easier one, because the reader is going to more than meet you halfway. Salespeople would describe such readers as "pre-sold" customers. Yet just as a good salesperson can ruin a deal by trying to convince the customer who's already sold to buy, you still need to consider your reader's specific needs. Clarity, precision of word choice, and flowing sentence structure remain of paramount importance, as do paragraph organization and the amount of background and supporting details. Also, don't overlook the need to explain technical terms and principles, even when writing to the most devoted lover of innovative software and electronic gadgetry. Interest alone often will not automatically enable the reader to understand technical concepts and details.

How Knowledgeable Is the Reader About My Topic?

Mark Twain observed, "We are all ignorant, but about different things." One mistake technical professionals make when writing for non-technical readers is assuming their readers are as knowledgeable as they are about the subject. This is a fatal assumption that will only result in confusion and frustration for your reader. Also, a great deal of your time will be spent generating additional messages to the reader trying to explain what should have been clear the first time. Just because it's clear to you does not make it clear to your reader. If you are an engineer or accountant writing to others in your field, then perhaps there will less need to explain all aspects of your message. If you're writing to the senior vice president of marketing, who is not familiar with software applications, then you will need to "walk" that reader through your message. Remember that when it comes to technical knowledge, writers and readers are hardly equal. So never talk down to your readers. Explain, yes; talk down, no. You will never be forgiven.

If you are asked to write instructions for operating dangerous equipment and you know the potential operators have little formal education, you would be wise to keep the writing as simple as possible. Short sentences. Perhaps illustrations. Explicit warnings. Now suppose you have to send a copy to your supervisor, who holds a Ph.D. in engineering. Do you write two versions? One simple and one more elaborate? Which of your readers is most important? The operators or the supervisor? The answer is that because the operators are the primary audience, the writing level and style need to be directed towards them. Obviously, you say, but beware of the tendency we all have to enjoy impressing family, friends, and coworkers with our knowledge. Keep in mind the need to write for your primary readers. Resist the temptation to write to impress the less important reader, no matter how high up the corporate management hierarchy.

If you have to write for multiple readers with different needs and levels of expertise, one helpful technique is to structure the writing content according to their particular needs. For instance, provide different summaries for reports or reverse the order of information and begin with the conclusions or recommendations or provide illustrations before presenting your discussion.

Are there additional potential readers?

Although you always write for your primary reader, you also need to consider potential additional readers. Your customer may forward your e-mail message or sales letter to his or her supervisor. Someone within your company may forward your e-mail to another department or to a senior manager. So it's important that even the most casual correspondence be well organized and clearly expressed. Nowadays, thanks to e-mail technology, there's less guarantee than ever that your business correspondence will be limited to your reader's eyes.

Does My Reader Have the Expertise to Understand the Content?

The less your reader knows, the more you need to explain. I have often heard business and technical professionals express annoyance at having to elaborate on what to them are simple statements or facts. Although frustration and impatience are understandable feelings, they will always prove counterproductive to effective written communication. You do not need to try, nor will you have the ability, to transform your readers into experts in your field. You do have to offer some guidance to help in them understand your key ideas, important statements, and observations. You might find it annoying to have to write the equivalent of "in other words..." but your ability to communicate clearly with your readers will depend upon it.

Do I Need to Provide Minimal or Substantial Background Information and Supporting Details?

Whenever we approach two people in the middle of a discussion, we usually do not interrupt or automatically begin talking. Not only would it be rude to do so, but it would also be disruptive to the flow of information being exchanged. Unless it's a matter of urgency, we wait until we get some idea of what they are discussing before attempting to contribute to that topic or we say nothing until there is a pause in the conversation.

Background information serves either as a point of departure for your message or to delay it interminably. How much do your readers need to know before they can understand your main ideas or the essence of your message? Be careful to avoid "overkill" (excessive data, facts, and figures) in your background details. The right amount of background information is similar to timing in comedy: Without it, the best of jokes will fall flat.

Should I Explain Technical Terms, Concepts, Abbreviations, and Acronyms?

The answer to this question is simple: Always explain any words, phrases, terms, acronyms, abbreviations, and technological jargon to any reader who may be unfamiliar with their meanings. Of course, providing a glossary of these terms will always be welcome by your readers. Another technique is to provide the definition within parentheses directly following the technical term. This practice allows your readers to sustain a relatively uninterrupted flow of information.

Would Illustrations Be Helpful?

Readers always welcome pictures, provided they are appropriate to the subject or helpful to understanding. Yet illustrations such as tables, line charts, and bar graphs alone often cannot convey meaning. You will find that one picture will not be worth two of the proverbial thousand words if it contains data and numbers and other details no one can understand nor be certain why it's there. So whenever you add illustrations, ask yourself if they can serve as stand-alone supplements to the text or if they require that you add some clarifying commentary, in addition.

Should I Include an Executive Summary of Key Points of Interest for Readers Who May Be Too Busy or Insufficiently Knowledgeable About My Topic?

For busy managers or executives, having to read less translates generally into more when it comes to their time. Summaries and abstracts, best placed at the beginning of your writing, will be welcome by all readers (busy or otherwise) because you are giving them the opportunity to gain an overview of the main message without having to pursue the details. Even in brief correspondence, readers will appreciate your including a summary. The value of a summary to your reader rests with your ability to emphasize the key points succinctly. The benefit of your providing a summary is the greater likelihood that your message will actually be read and its main ideas clearly understood.

Are There Any Actions the Reader or Organization Needs to Take? If So, What Are They? When and How Should They Be Taken?

Don't be a mystery writer when it comes to requesting your readers take action. Suspense is fine for thriller novels and adventure movies but not for business writing. Don't hedge when it comes to telling your readers when and why you need their immediate response to a problem or question, to submit a report, or to complete a questionnaire by a specific date. Avoid being too blunt in requesting action, but also remember that what's convenient for one person may be unimportant for another.

An important consideration is your knowing what the reader doesn't want or need. Some busy managers find summaries helpful or want to see only your conclusions and recommendations; others want a wealth of technical details, while others simply want to know how to use the new software and whom to call when something goes wrong. Remember that although your readers' needs, expectations, and preferences may vary, one element does not: the desire to be able to understand your message without the need for an interpreter.

What's the Point?

Perhaps the first question to ask yourself is this: What should the writing accomplish? The answer will most likely be one of the following most common goals:

- Provide or request information.
- Outline instructions or procedures.
- Explain or justify decisions and actions.
- Motivate a reader to decide or act.
- Persuade the reader to understand or accept the writer's viewpoint or position.
- Document results of work assignments or tasks.
- Evaluate individual or group performance.

Identifying your purpose for writing is essential to engage the reader's interest and understanding. You have to ask why you are writing in the first place. What is the goal? What is the point? Is it to propose a solution to a problem? Offer instruction for using the new software? Provide recommendations for improving customer service? Pacify an angry client? Request approval of a new procedure? Suggest action or obtain compliance? Knowing the purpose makes your job easier because it provides you and your reader with direction and focus. You never want your reader to ask: "Why did you write to me?" Your purpose should be apparent in the first sentence, paragraph, report title, or e-mail subject line.

Example

In the following memo, the writer has not effectively emphasized its purpose.

TO: Cynthia Avon, Senior V-P, Operations
FROM: Dick Dawson
SUBJECT: Utilizing Energy

Last spring we decided to reduce energy utilization by 5 percent. We have lately met that goal. Our organization grew by 9 percent this year. A survey of operations indicated that additional reductions in energy utilization will be very difficult to achieve. In consideration of the ever-growing cost of energy, our organization faces an energy conservation dilemma. Utilization of energy will grow because of increased use of technology such as computers and automated equipment. Also, we are installing larger

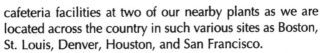

cafeteria facilities at two of our nearby plants as we are located across the country in such various sites as Boston, St. Louis, Denver, Houston, and San Francisco.

Bearing this background information in mind, I would appreciate your either scheduling a meeting or authorizing me to do so to discuss the impact of future utilization and conservation of energy at our operations sites and some of my suggestions for reducing costs. If you require additional background information, I will be happy to provide it. Thank you.

Example Revised With a Clear Statement of Purpose

TO: Cynthia Avon, Senior V-P, Operations

FROM: Dick Dawson

SUBJECT: Meeting to Discuss Future Energy Needs and Costs

Although we have succeeded this year in reducing energy utilization by 5 percent, a survey of operations indicates that additional reductions will be difficult to achieve due to increased use of information technology and automated equipment. Given the ever-growing cost of energy, I would appreciate meeting with you to discuss several energy-conserving suggestions likely to reduce future energy costs at our various national operations centers.

The Basic Roadmap

Transforming notes and observations into sentences and paragraphs that will form the first draft will be less stressful if you do the following:

1. Begin with a topic sentence or paragraph informing the reader of your subject, what you want to say and why. This sentence is similar to the headline sentence in a newspaper or magazine article. For example:

    A recent survey conducted among corporate managers reveals general agreement of the role business needs to play in providing training opportunities for all levels of personnel.

2. Next, provide details to support or clarify your initial statement or position. These details can be brief or elaborate, depending your purpose and reader's needs. For example:

   In the last five years, the managers of Corporate Training Departments who responded to the survey offered more than 100 seminars in management development, written and spoken communications skills, leadership roles, time management, strategic planning, and computer and software instruction to employees.

3. The conclusion or closing serves to complete your message and provide a sense of unity to the preceding details. Closings include recommendations, solutions, and calls for action. Do not introduce new ideas, questions, or other information outside the scope of your opening or main idea sentence and supporting details. Your closing must complete your thoughts; your readers must feel as satisfied with your ending as those of a well-plotted mystery or Hollywood love story. The reader must never feel that something is missing, unexplained, or unexpressed. Here's an example:

   Managers agreed that after attending various internal training programs, participants displayed increased confidence, enhanced productivity, and improved job performance.

Visualize Your Writing

Perhaps you might find it helpful to think of your message in terms of three sentences or paragraphs enclosed within a pyramid. At the top is the main idea statement or opening providing focus and direction to your reader. Following are supporting factual details, numerical data, or professional opinions, listed in order of importance or relevance. At the base are concluding thoughts, recommendations, or closing comments. However you decide to proceed, remember the writing is not for your eyes only, but expressly for those of your reader.

4

The Right Package: Organizing and Evaluating Information

*"If any man wish to write in a clear style,
let him be first clear in his thoughts."*
—Johann Wolfgang von Goethe

ALL WRITING IS AN ATTEMPT to impose a sense of order on the chaotic random flow of impressions and ideas swirling about in our minds. From the simplest e-mail message to the most detailed report, the task all writers face is how to best organize and present the information to their readers. Yet how do you accomplish this feat? To begin you need to ask questions about the data and details you collect. If the writing has a beginning, middle, and ending, would using traditional sentence and paragraph format prove best? Perhaps lists or a series of illustrations supported by minimal textual explanation would do. Should you provide a summary or list the conclusions and recommendations in the beginning rather than the end? All writers face these considerations and questions. How can the major ideas be readily distinguished from the minor ones? What is likely to be of interest to the reader? What facts or figures will hold your reader's attention?

Divide and Conquer

One helpful technique is to separate the information into primary and secondary categories. What does the reader need to know? What information is of major importance? Next, you need to evaluate the information according to its purpose. Does it serve as a main idea, supporting detail, conclusion, or recommendation? Then, select the details that will support, explain, illustrate, or highlight the key ideas and contribute directly to the development of your message.

Let's say you need to prepare a report for a software manufacturer about the market potential of a specific program designed to enhance the critical-thinking and problem-solving skills of managers. You've gathered a great deal of information about different types of on-line training programs (their purposes, advantages and disadvantages, limitations, costs, and sales performance). Additionally, assume you have collected a number of market surveys outlining the potential needs among various types of businesses for such an on-line training program, have interviewed various individuals in business and in educational software design, and have received written replies and statements from various parties regarding the need and potential appeal of the program.

Now, keeping the report's purpose in mind—the market potential of a specific program designed to enhance the critical thinking and problem-solving skills of managers—you decide to focus the report primarily on the written statements gathered from various sources because those comments will serve as the strongest support for your proposal. Although the information about different types of on-line training programs will be of interest to your reader, you decide to summarize key facts in an opening statement and place everything else in an appendix, because this data (advantages and disadvantages, costs, and sales performance of the programs) will either provide only secondary support for your proposal or prove digressive. You must resist the temptation to include the information you've gathered simply because considerable time was spent in doing so. Otherwise, forcing unnecessary information on your readers will be oppressive rather than convincing.

Analyze the Content and Function

Information can be organized according to its content and intended function. You will find it helpful to consider material in terms of such patterns as chronological development or time order, cause and effect, problem and solution, comparison and contrast, fact and opinion, description, definition, and example.

For instance, if you are writing a project status report, you would need to consider which information best conveys development or progress according to time and accomplished tasks. After grouping the information according to topic or purpose, you can then determine which material would serve best in an introduction, main body of discussion, conclusion, or recommendations. Use the following traditional patterns of organization to help you "package" information for your readers.

Time Order

If you are writing a trip report, instructions, procedures, or an incident and/or progress report in which the sequence of events or activities is central to your purpose, present the information according to order of sequence and occurrence. Helpful words include *first, next, then, after, following,* and *last.*

Example:

On March 1, Livingston Wingate, president of PB Information Systems, suggested that in-house training programs for management and support personnel be expanded to meet the increasing challenges of the new decade. The following day, Mr. Wingate assigned responsibility for all training programs to Thurston Martin, Director of Human Resources. Mr. Martin then asked his assistant, Geraldine Olson, to prepare a report on current training needs. Ms. Olson completed her report within two weeks. Mr. Martin reviewed the report before submitting it to Mr. Wingate, who immediately had copies distributed to all senior managers.

Spatial Order

If your focus is on physical description, you need to enable the reader to "see" as clearly as if you provided a picture. Words and phrases such as *above, below, near, adjacent, vertical or horizontal to, in the center, above and below,* and *to the right or left* will help your reader focus as clearly on your subject as the very best of digital cameras would allow.

Example:

The general reception area is in urgent need of redecorating. The space between the entry doors is so narrow that two people cannot pass each other at the same time. There are soil spots on the floor. The white paint above the receptionist's desk has yellowed and is peeling. Last week several small pieces fell on a client's head. Behind the desk is an open window that permits anyone to see employees playing cards or watching television. On the wall to the left are several black-framed portraits of executives who have been deceased for 50 years. Below the portraits is a long brown sofa with several torn areas patched with orange tape. Next to the sofa is a small wooden table whose top is scratched and is covered with coffee stains. Above the table a long diagonal crack appears in the wall. Attached to the wall on the right are two stuffed fierce-looking snakes that appear poised to attack the next visitor.

Cause and Effect

Now here is the truth of Isaac Newton's law of motion (that every action has a reaction) more helpful than in using this pattern to develop your message. You can either present the causes or effects first, depending upon which will have the greater importance or interest to your reader.

Example:

Based on recent studies regarding the expected rise in the number of aging Americans, especially among those members of the Baby Boomer generation (1946–1964), toy industry sources are optimistic about the possibility for long-term growth. The Bureau of the Census has projected that the rise in the elderly population will increase dramatically in the next 10 years. Toy industry sources expect that of the millions retiring, a substantial number of aging Americans will no doubt enter a second childhood. This in turn, they believe, will enlarge the primary market for toys and games in the next two decades.

Comparison and Contrast

Noting the similarities and differences is particularly helpful when you have to weigh the advantages and disadvantages of two or more products, services, ideas, proposals, solutions, or theories. You need to review each item according to similar comparative criteria, such as cost, effectiveness, function, benefits, practicality, location, size, and any other distinguishing characteristic or feature.

Example:

Sales of sporting goods and recreational equipment this year are expected to increase 25 percent from consumer purchases last year. The sporting industry produces a wide variety of equipment. The most important in terms of dollar value are pleasure boats, sports footwear, hunting equipment, bicycles and supplies, and exercise equipment. The remainder consists of items such as equipment, clothing, and supplies used in numerous other activities, ranging from bowling, tennis, and racquetball to archery and snow and water skiing. Projected sales compared with the previous category are expected to be strong but generally lower.

Additional Patterns

Following are alternative methods of organization for e-mail, letters, memos, and reports:

Method 1

- Statement of Problem.
- Background.
- Analysis of Causes.
- Possible Solutions.
- Recommendation.

Method 2

- Summary.
- Background.
- Introductory Statement.
- Description of Equipment.
- Discussion of Operating Procedures.
- Conclusion.

Method 3

- Recommendations, Conclusions, Findings.
- Topic Statement.
- Background.
- Discussion of Details.

Method 4

- Summary.
- Statement of Problem.
- Background.
- Analysis of Problem.

Head vs. Heart:
Evaluating the Information

We are often advised to think with our heads and feel with our hearts. However, if you live long enough, you learn that this wisdom is far easier to express verbally than to follow. No matter how we may resist, our thinking can easily become clouded or influenced by our emotions. Of course it does, you might say. After all, we're not machines, and who hasn't experienced times when emotions affected our critical thinking and judgment? How often are we advised that if "it doesn't feel right," whether for a relationship or new shoes, something is wrong. The same advice may be true for writing. If we think too much with our hearts, we might soon regret what we write. Worse, the writing will suffer for not being expressed with the clear-minded objectivity it (and your reader) required. Perhaps you will find it helpful to bear in mind these questions designed to offset the strong influence emotions often have on critical perspective:

1. Have I presented mostly a series of generalizations unsupported by specific details or data?
2. Did I allow the writing to be influenced by any preexisting notions and opinions?
3. Have I assumed the reader will accept an idea as being true simply because I say so?
4. Have I misread or misinterpreted facts to support my point of view?
5. Does the information support one of many interpretations? If so, have I presented all of them?
6. What conclusions tend to emerge both repeatedly and irrefutably?

Pitfalls to Accurate Evaluation of Information

Remember to be aware of these common pitfalls to accurate, objective interpretation of information.

Generalizations

Generalizations are similar to stereotypes. In the stereotype there exists one small kernel of truth, but that truth does

---

 Quick Guide to Organizing Information

Organization in writing consists of:

*   *Sorting out* from the collected data the essential information the reader will need.
*   *Developing sentences* to convey this information.
*   *Grouping these sentences* into a series of paragraphs that develop main ideas.
*   *Arranging the paragraphs* into an overall pattern that shows their relationship to one another and ultimately leads to a conclusion.

not tell the whole tale. Relying on that one little truth to reach a conclusion distorts the whole truth. In writing, relying on sweeping generalizations alone is likely to undermine your credibility. Oddly enough, in fact, generalizations are a necessary starting point for stating an overview of your basic message. For example:

> There are indications that business is improving.
> Cindy wants to bake a chocolate cake for Dick.

The challenge for the first statement will be to add supporting facts consisting of numerical data, such as recent sales figures, surveys of consumer buying trends, and factual proof of additional or resurgent interest in your company's products or services (possibly including professional opinions from sales representatives and buyers to support sales or production data). For Cindy's cake, she will soon have to acquire the essential cooking ingredients and utensils before proceeding. So although generalizations can serve as initial foundations of thought, they can never serve as conclusive ones as well without hard, supporting evidence.

Assumptions and Inferences

If you have ever misinterpreted someone's remark or comment (and who hasn't?) and later had to apologize with "But I thought you meant..." you well understand the dangers inherent in drawing conclusions by way of inference. The tendency we all have to interpret information or draw conclusions via assumptions and inferences reminds me of the well-known expression to never judge a book by its cover. Information and appearances can be all too deceiving. The man you see driving an expensive sports car may or may not be rich enough to afford it. The car might be rented or may belong to his brother-in-law.

Assumptions and inferences are drawn from whatever information is presumed to be accurate at first glance. This in turn leads to drawing conclusions based on what is suggested or perceived rather than directly stated or proven to be factual evidence. Similar to generalizations, inferences can be a helpful first step to the extent they point us in an initial direction of possible reasons or solutions for problems or of the relationships among ideas. The danger of relying solely on assumptions and inferences is the likelihood of their pointing us (and ultimately our readers) in the wrong direction.

Begging the Question

This pitfall occurs when you readily accept an unproven premise or statement as being true. For example:

> I don't think our firm should invest in such a poorly managed company.

Further research and investigation may prove that the company in question encountered difficulties for reasons other than poor management.

Faulty Analogy

This error in reasoning occurs when two ideas with little in common are compared and when it is assumed that if two objects are similar in *some* ways, they are equal in *all* ways. For example:

> Oversized SUVs may one day go the way of dinosaurs.
>
> Lauren will make a fine bank president because she is an accountant.

Perhaps SUVs will become obsolete, but not for the same reasons as dinosaurs. How does Lauren's knowledge of accounting ensure her competency as a bank president?

Non Sequitur ("It does not follow.")

This common error in reasoning results from the assumption improperly drawn and expressed. For example:

a. Computer manufacturers are losing money.
b. IBM manufactures computers.
c. IBM is losing money.

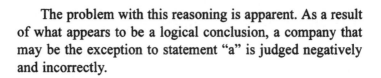

The problem with this reasoning is apparent. As a result of what appears to be a logical conclusion, a company that may be the exception to statement "a" is judged negatively and incorrectly.

Evaluation Checklist

Answering the following questions will help you accurately assess the information you need to present to your reader:

1. How much of the information I have gathered is truly relevant to the purpose and scope of my communication?
2. Have I gathered enough information to address the major issues?
3. How reliable are the facts? Are they numerically accurate? Have I double-checked the source of these facts?
4. Are the facts recent or dated?
5. Do the opinions expressed by various individuals relate to the central topic?
6. Are any opinions self-serving?
7. Is there any indication of personal bias?
8. Were the opinions expressed by experts?
9. Have I documented all sources of information for future reference and accountability?
10. Have I exhausted major sources of information?
11. Have I compared items that do not have a basis for comparison?
12. Have I properly emphasized opinions, numerical data, and other pertinent details?
13. Have I organized the information in a logical sequence and in order of importance?
14. Have I drawn false conclusions or overgeneralized ones?
15. Are all conclusions and recommendations fully emphasized?

Problem-Solving Techniques

A great deal of business writing involves addressing and solving problems. As a result, you may be called upon to determine, analyze, and offer solutions to one or more problems. Although the nature of the problems will vary, their solutions will always require clear thinking and a methodical approach. Also necessary is your ability to resist the tendency to overlook information that is contrary to previously held notions and personal biases. Otherwise you will be expressing a collection of subjective opinions rather than an objective report. A series of problem-solving questions that can help you identify and address any problem in an effective manner follows:

To Define the Existing or Anticipated Problem, Ask These Questions:

- What is the specific problem or difficulty?
- Who or what is being affected by the problem?
- Why is the problem occurring?
- What are the precise causes of the problem?
- How can the problem be corrected or at least diminished?

To Decide if the Problem Has a Major or Minor Cause, Ask These Questions:

- Is the cause simple or complex, obvious or vague?
- Can the cause be easily and quickly corrected?

To Offer Solutions to the Problem, Ask These Questions:

- What kind of solution would prove most effective?
- Will the solution require a reasonable amount of money, time, ingenuity, or physical effort?
- Can the solution be easily implemented? Is it practical?

- What chance does the solution have of succeeding?
- Is the solution immediately applicable?
- Will the solution be temporary or permanent?
- Will there be any resistance by management or other key individuals?
- Is the solution likely to create an additional problem?
- If there are several solutions available, have I weighed their advantages and disadvantages?

Guidelines for Addressing Problems

When attempting to discuss problems and offer possible solutions, following these guidelines will prove helpful:

1. DEFINE the key problem as you perceive it.
2. DISTINGUISH actual problems from causes and solutions.

    Do not offer the solution first: We need to improve customer-service procedures.

    Define the problem: We are receiving increasing complaints about customer service.
3. CONSIDER who, what, where, when, why, how, and to what extent.
4. SPECIFY causes of the problem.
5. PRESENT alternative solutions.
6. SUGGEST the best course of action or solution in your view.

Complex Problems

Complex problems often have more than one cause. A series of forces or conditions is usually at work. Your difficulty when writing is to decide which of the several suspected or probable causes are truly responsible for the problem. For example, consider this:

Mel Markey was promoted to manager because he sold more computers than all other salespersons. His success in sales was surely due to his good looks, which appealed to female customers.

The reason for Mel's success may have something to do with the information expressed in the second sentence. Yet other factors may account for his success, such as his ability to inspire trust; his thorough knowledge of the various products; his pleasant, patient, and respectful attitude towards his customers; and his willingness to address any complaints or service problems. Moreover, additional factors most likely contributed to his being promoted. Mel may have always been routinely helpful to his sales associates, frequently consulted for advice and product information, asked to train new employees, and ultimately given greater responsibility, all culminating in his being rewarded with a new title and higher salary. Because all these factors are never addressed in the initial statement, its credibility is clearly questionable.

Getting Physical: Designing the Document

Noise pollution can take many forms. In writing, one of the foremost sources of unappreciated noise actually doesn't make a sound yet can become unbearably deafening. You may have often heard that typing an e-mail or other correspondence in all caps "shouts" your message to your readers. Perhaps this is so, because the mere size alone of every letter trumpets its importance. Just as in other matters, bigger is not necessarily better, the same applies to typeface size and selection.

The true problem with trying to read all caps is just that: It's difficult. A line or two, perhaps even a short paragraph, is fine when you want to emphasize an idea or express a warning. Otherwise, ever since we were in grade school we learned to read in upper- and lowercase. As adults we continue this practice, and so do the major newspapers, textbooks, journals, and magazines we read. Even comic book dialogue is printed in upper- and lowercase. Also, typing words in all caps makes primary information indistinguishable from the rest of the text, supporting and secondary details. What's of major importance?

What's not? On the other hand, typing words in all lowercase suggests that little or nothing is really of much importance. Remember those proverbial English teachers who said that anyone who writes the pronoun "i" in lowercase doesn't have much self-esteem? Whatever your thoughts about the truth of that belief, typing in all upper- or lower-case indicates laziness or selfish disregard for the reader.

Typeface

Choosing the right type and size will produce correspondence that is easily read and understood. As in all other art and design, in writing form follows function. There are two types of typefaces:

- Serif: M
- Sans serif: M

Serif fonts, such as Times New Roman, are easier to read for general text than sans serif.

Example:

Good morning, Tom.

It was good to hear from you and that you are planning to visit San Francisco this fall. Martha Grace and I are looking forward to seeing you again.

Sans serif typefaces work best in headings, brief announcements, large display and signs, and any information that needs to be highlighted.

Example:

PERSONAL PROTECTION EQUIPMENT MUST BE WORN BEFORE ENTERING LAB.

Typeface may be mixed for contrast between text and headings, but do so with caution because not all typefaces mix well.

Typeface Size (Point)

I am always amazed and amused by the writer who shows me a one-page memo, letter, or report and proudly announces, "I got all three pages onto one." My response usually is, "Great, but who can read it?" Don't make this mistake. Although your reader may be more apt to want to read a one-page memo, the size of typeface you choose will affect the readability of your document. Do not try to squeeze all the information onto one page in an effort to economize or provide an incentive for reading. No reader will go beyond a line or two if the text is so small it causes eyestrain. On the other hand, type that is too large is also difficult to read.

This is fine for signs but not for reports.

In general, a 10 or 12 point typeface will suffice.

Line Length

It is best to keep your line length below 64 characters to ensure readability. Otherwise, there is a tendency for readers to lose their place.

Margins

Do not feel that you have to justify margins at both ends. Feel free to align text on the left and leave the right "ragged."

Paragraph Length

One way to avoid creating large blocks of paragraphs is to list information in bullet form whenever possible, especially if the information is a sequence of details or series of procedures. For example, instead of writing:

Accumulated sick leave is granted to all employees when they are unable to perform their duties because of sickness, injury, pregnancy, and confinement, or for medical, dental, optical examination or treatment, or when a member of the immediate family is afflicted with an illness that requires the attendance of the employee, or when through exposure to contagious disease, the presence of the employee at his or her post would jeopardize the health of others.

Provide the information as a list:

Accumulated sick leave is granted to all employees when they are unable to perform their duties because of:

- Sickness, injury, pregnancy, and confinement.
- Medical, dental, optical examination or treatment.
- A member of the immediate family is afflicted with an illness that requires the attendance of the employee.
- Exposure to contagious disease, where the presence of the employee at his or her post would jeopardize the health of others.

 7 Guidelines for the Emphasis of Key Ideas

1. Use headings to highlight key ideas and larger sections of information.
2. Place key ideas in opening and closing paragraphs.
3. Repeat and summarize main ideas.
4. Place secondary or minor information in an appendix or footnote.
5. Place additional white space around text and within tables to achieve greater visual appeal and emphasis.
6. Present important details in lists rather than sentences and paragraphs.
7. Use various fonts, point sizes, underlining, bold face, color, italics, and capital letters to highlight major topics of discussion.

5

Don't Obfuscate:
Writing With Clarity and Precision

> Polonius: *"What do you read, my lord?"*
> Hamlet: *"Words, words, words."*

IMAGINE RECEIVING THIS MESSAGE FROM your friendly insurance company:

> The purpose of this letter is to provide information you requested regarding there is in existence a grace period regarding payment of said medical insurance policy. Please be advised that the aforementioned is of a duration of 10 days following premium due date previously established at the outset of said policy.

How would you react? What curses might you mutter? Would you need to lie down because you suddenly feel dizzy? Probably both. It's hard to believe such sentences could have been created by a living breathing person for another person to read. Who could ever imagine such wording was intended to express this simple message:

> After the due date, your medical insurance policy allows a 10-day grace period to submit payment.

It is difficult to imagine any writer deliberately setting out to confuse the reader. So why would anyone want to write such a baffling message? Probably for the same reason the newly rich person believes it essential to drive a fancy expensive car or live in an oversized mansion: how else to display his or her newly acquired wealth for all to see? Just as old moneyed folks usually own ordinary cars that do not call attention to themselves, so too must writers understand that there is no need to call attention to the writing as writing. There is even less need to "hit the reader over the head" with obscure vocabulary or long-winded sentences.

Talk Is Cheap: Show Me the Cash

The Bible offers this wise advice for writers: "Let thy words be few." The modern variant of *less is more* in writing is one of the surest guidelines to successful written communication. Less for its own sake is not the goal here; rather, it serves as a touchstone. No writer should ever be brief at the expense of leaving out important details or other data. At the same time, I can't imagine anyone arriving at work on a Monday morning, finding a 500-page report on his or her desk, and commenting, "I can't wait to read this." Most likely the comment would be: "Who put this on my desk?" or "Do I really have to read all this?"

Words: The Tools of the Trade

If words are the tools or building blocks of our language, then the success of your writing will always depend on the words you choose to convey your thoughts. Words function primarily to express, not impress. Words are created to convey meaning, not to advertise an extensive vocabulary. Perhaps the idea of obtaining an impressive vocabulary all begins as we make our way from grade school through high school to college. We are encouraged to expand our vocabularies to become better readers, writers, speakers, listeners, and scrabble players. This is all fine. At the same time, we need to remember that writing is not a game show where whoever uses the fanciest or most obscure words wins the prize. The goal is to enable the reader to fully understand our message, not to find our vocabulary impressive. Our words need to convey the substance of our messages, not the shadows.

Mark Twain confessed, "I never write metropolis if paid the same amount to write city." So why would you? Yet despite Twain's sensible approach to word choice, I'm not suggesting that simple or familiar words alone will carry the day for you. Even as simple a sentence as this obviously conveys more than the writer intended:

Eat Here and Get Gas

Rather, you have to achieve a balanced meaning among your choice of words:

All *components* are included.

But when it comes to sentences containing what I perceive as "overbaked" expressions, think twice:

We need to *effectuate improvement*
of our training procedures.

Wouldn't this sentence do just fine?

We need *to improve* our training procedures.

An unfamiliar word or expression achieves only two results: Your reader must consult a dictionary before continuing and, worse, the communication process has been interrupted.

When choosing your words, try to prefer those that are:

- *Familiar* to most readers (*limits* vs. parameters).
- *Specific* (*call, meet, send* vs. get back).
- *Economical* (*assist, help* vs. provide every assistance).

NOTE: Always consider your reader's ability or limitations for understanding technical words, jargon, and acronyms before using them. It may be best to limit their use or to provide a glossary.

Reader-Friendly Words

If you've ever attended a party and were told to dress casually but showed up wearing business attire whereas everyone else was in shorts and sneakers, you probably began to feel not only uncomfortable but wondered if you received the same invitation. Most likely you spent the evening or afternoon commenting to everyone, "Nobody told me to wear shorts and sneakers." The list on the facing page is offered as a guide to avoid "overdressed" writing. The list is intended to serve as a source of comparison; word choice is ultimately a question of style and individual preference. As in other aspects of life, there is no accounting for poor taste, pretense, and pomposity in business writing, however unintentional. As Shakespeare's Hamlet once advised a group of actors, "Suit the action to the word, the word to the action."

Underdressed Words

The list on the facing page provides you with alternative word choices for expressions that are either verbose or border on the pretentious. Their common use clearly indicates writers' mistaken notions of how written English phrases should "sound" to impress their readers. The result is that some words and expressions arrive overdressed for the occasion. Yet words can often be underdressed. Writing the way we speak is fine as long as it fits the purpose of the message and doesn't cross the invisible line in the reader's mind that distinguishes the acceptable word from the inappropriate one. You'll find a list of familiar casual expressions and their alternative counterparts on page 58.

The Devil Made Me Do It

Think of how many times you use the word *make* in conversational speech. You could "make a big deal of" something or "make a long trip" next summer or "make a cake." Who would argue with our employing such an often used word in our business writing? In most instances the reader would argue, especially if you used "make" to create an

Wordy	Concise
accomplish the project	complete, finish
afford an opportunity	allow, permit, enable
attached/enclosed herewith please find	attached/enclosed is/are
at an early date of time	soon
based on the fact that	because
deem	believe, think, consider
due to the fact that	due to, because
during the time that	during, when
effect modifications	modify, change, endeavor, attempt, try
finalize	conclude
for the purpose of	for, to
furnish	provide, send
in addition to the above	also
in the amount of	for
in close proximity to	near
in the event that	if
in a position to	can, able
interpose no objections	agree with
involve the necessity of	involve
is found to be	is
make an adjustment to	adjust
make mention of	mention, make reference to, refer
perform an analysis of	analyze
predicated upon	based upon
present a conclusion	conclude
pursuant to	according to, by
pursuant to your request	as you requested
raise the question	ask
take under consideration	consider
through the use of	by, with
we are in receipt of	we received
with the exception of	except for

Instead of:	Use:
about-face	reverse
about to	ready
back to square one	begin again
bottom line	main thought
bring up	introduce
brush up on	review
by and large	in general
call on	visit
carry the ball	be responsible
check over	examine, review, come across, discover
come up with	create, design
cut out	remove, delete
deal with	address, confront
drop off	deliver
figure on	plan, expect
get in touch with	phone, visit, write
go over	review, examine
hand in	submit, provide
hinge on	depend on
hold up	delay
how come	why
keep in mind	remember
put off	postpone, suspend
run across	meet
turn out	produce, happen
wipe out	eliminate

expression that could have been conveyed through a single word. On the facing page is a list of expressions beginning with "make" that we all use in everyday speech but that will hardly be welcome by our readers. Although there's nothing wrong with writing these longer expressions in our first drafts, reducing them to their single-word forms during the editing stage will improve the rhythmic flow of your sentences.

"Make" expressions	Single-word expressions
make an estimation of	estimate
make a report to	report
make a study of	study
make a decision to	decide
make a drawing of	draw
make a list of	list
make an examination of	examine
make a preference of	prefer
make an approximation of	approximate
make the acquaintance of	meet
make an evaluation of	evaluate
make a trip to	travel
make an observation	observe
make a disturbance	disturb
make a nuisance of	annoy
make a reference to	refer
make a point of	point to, emphasize
make a phone call	telephone, phone
make an improvement	improve
make an objection	object
make a calculation	calculate
make a notation	note
make a repair	repair
make a request	request
make a correction	correct
make a suggestion	suggest
make a payment	pay
make a return	return
make a collection	collect

Redundant Words and Expressions

If you were charged twice for the same item the next time you shopped at your local supermarket, you would not be happy. In writing, the same holds true when you use redundant words and expressions. You're writing it twice and the reader is reading it twice. What's the point? Emphasis?

Perhaps, especially in speech when we want to underscore an idea. More likely we hear and see those words so often we come to think they're fine. A list on the facing page shows the more common ones you would do well to avoid writing.

You Can't Buy Class: Euphemisms

All the money in the world can buy fancy clothes, fine furniture, and exotic cars, but it can't buy class. That's never for sale, but something you're born with or acquire instinctively as a result of your own innate good taste and sense of style. The same rule applies to the words we choose. Unless you're Woody Allen, you'd probably never get away with wearing sneakers with a tuxedo. Yet that's just what writers try to do when using words that don't fit the occasion, are overly formal, or worse, are intended to hide the true meaning of their message.

Euphemisms are expressions that serve to transform an offensive or tactless words or references into inoffensive and agreeable ones ("physically challenged" for "crippled"). Politically correct terms are euphemisms designed as acceptable substitutions for rude, insulting, and archaic ones ("Native American" for "Indian"). Euphemisms can also hide seemingly simple and straightforward words behind deceptive or overly complex ones ("downsize" for "layoff"). Euphemisms often assume a strained quality, as if trying too hard. For example, you are attending a party and the host asks, "May I bring you a *libation?*"there's a good chance you will respond with a quizzical look or perhaps laugh outright, resulting in your not getting anything to drink because your host has responded by demanding you leave immediately!

Euphemisms can dress up an embarrassing or awkward situation or disguise a negative one. For example:

> The company experienced a *net profits revenue deficiency* this quarter.

Avoid:	Instead, Use:
absolutely nothing	nothing
advance forward	advance
and also	(either word)
assemble together	assemble
at the present time	at present, now
attach together	attach
basic and fundamental	(either word)
brief in duration	brief
but nevertheless	(either word)
circle around	circle
close proximity	near
continue on	continue
cooperate together	cooperate
descend down	descend
disappear from sight	disappear
during the time	during, when
each and every one	each, every one
empty out	empty
end result	result
exactly the same	the same
first and foremost	(either word)
fewer in number	fewer
following after	(either word)
give an estimate of	estimate
green in color	green
in the amount of	for
in the state of New York	New York
large in size	large
neat in appearance	neat
plan ahead	plan
reduce down	reduce
resume again	resume
return back	return
round in shape	round
seven in number	seven
thanks and appreciation	(either word)
true fact	fact
universal the world over	universal
very unique	unique

In other words, the company lost a lot of money.

Or euphemisms can dress up a plain old used car by advertising it as *pre-owned* or a cemetery for your dearly departed pet as a *memory garden*. So why do people use words and expressions that inhibit their messages? Perhaps because using them makes us feel important or we imagine the fancy words and expressions will convey our intelligence, educational background, or professional ability without doubt to our readers. Yet language should not call attention to itself for the sake of attraction alone. Instead of the broad gestures and flourishes of the stage actor in a revival of a 17th-century French farce, perhaps word preference should be similar to the subtlety used by the most skillful of film actors. Eighteenth-century poet Alexander Pope expressed this view:

"Words are like leaves, and where they most abound, much fruit of sense beneath is rarely found."

Here is a brief list of some common euphemisms and their meanings. For an up-to-date list, simply consult any newspaper or magazine or pay attention to the next political, military, corporate, legal, or academic announcement you hear on television or radio.

Euphemism	Meaning
access controller	doorman
altercation	fight
directive	memo
facility	building
patron	customer
perpetrator	criminal
peruse	read
sanitary engineer	garbage collector
visual surveillance	spying

Familiarity Breeds Contempt: Cliches

We use cliches every day in our speech. These expressions are colorful and often appealing in their economy and ability to convey an image or description of an emotion or situation. Someone may be "green with envy" or "cold as ice" or "busy as a bee." A story may be "too funny for words." Similar to redundant expressions, cliches in speech do little harm. In writing, cliches suffer the fate occasioned when the familiar becomes contemptible. Your reader has heard and read these expressions so often they tend to "bounce off" the reader so swiftly they lose their appeal. Cliches in business writing ultimately diminish the strength and effectiveness of your message.

Here are some commonly used cliches:

- Between a rock and a hard place.
- Bark up the wrong tree.
- Carry the ball.
- This day and age.
- After all is said and done.
- Burn the midnight oil.
- On the ball.
- By leaps and bounds.
- Slowly but surely.
- Better late than never.
- Last but not least.

When in Rome: Regional Words and Expressions

The first time I visited a Chicago restaurant, I asked the waitress what kind of soda was offered. She answered, "We have seltzer or club." She must have noticed the dumb expression because she quickly added, "Do you want a Coke or some other pop instead?" In the Midwest, the regional term for a soft drink such as a Coke or root beer is *pop,* but I didn't know that. In my travels I soon learned that if you order coffee "regular" anywhere other than New York, the waiter will ask you to clarify your order. You might have to explain you want your coffee with cream and sugar.

Word	Definition
beignet	French-style donut (New Orleans)
binder	rubber band (Minnesota)
Cape Codder	cranberry juice and vodka (New England)
cork ball	baseball (St. Louis)
crank up the car	start the car (South Carolina/Georgia)
dinner	midday meal (North Carolina)
ground hackey	chipmunk (Pennsylvania)
hippen	diaper (Tennessee)
later	goodbye (Maine)
pop	soft drink (Chicago and elsewhere)
sleep in	oversleep (Pittsburgh)
hero	sandwich on Italian or French bread (New York)
sub	sandwich (Boston)
grinder	sandwich (Rhode Island)
hoagie	sandwich (Pennsylvania)
po' boy	sandwich (Texas and Georgia)
soda	soft drink (New York)
tadpoles	people (Mississippi)
thundering herd	pot of beans (Texas)
tolerable	fairly well (North Carolina)
truck room	storage room (Pennsylvania Dutch country)
unsweetened	no sugar, usually in iced tea (the South)

In the Brooklyn neighborhood of my childhood, we always used the expression *Italian heroes* for sandwiches we ordered for lunch, but in other parts of the country the term is *sub, hoagie,* or *grinder.* The first time I taught a seminar in Minneapolis some participants approached me at lunchtime and asked, "Do you want to come with?" to which I confusingly responded, "Go with? Where?" In the deep South, people may be *fixing to* do some chore or refer to someone as *bragging on* something rather than *bragging about.*

All of these are examples of regionalisms, words and expressions particular to a specific geographic region in the United

States. These regional expressions are often colorful, humorous, or imaginative constructions. Remembering to avoid using these terms in daily business writing is not an issue of correctness but of occasioning confusion among your readers. When writing casual messages within your company, you may choose to routinely use a regional expression. In fact, many writers are not aware the expressions they may use have geographic limitations in terms of meaning. When writing elsewhere in the country, it is best to use standard English expressions. A list of regional expressions appears on page 64.

Action Words

Use these words to convey strength, control, and confidence.

accomplish	eliminate	investigate	recommend
act	enable	lead	reduce
approve	establish	maintain	restore
assign	examine	manage	restructure
assist	expedite	moderate	revise
clarify	facilitate	monitor	revitalize
complete	formulate	motivate	shape
conduct	generate	negotiate	solve
contribute	guide	organize	streamline
control	identify	perform	strengthen
create	implement	permit	supervise
demonstrate	improve	plan	train
develop	initiate	produce	trim
direct	influence	provide	

A Word to the Wise

With respect to word choice, perhaps the comic writer James Thurber said it best:

"A word to the wise is insufficient if it makes no sense."

6

Leave Out the Commercials: Let the Sentences Sell the Message

"The love of economy is the root of all virtue."
—George Bernard Shaw

COMMERCIALS ON TELEVISION OR THE radio can be viewed as either clever, entertaining, and informative or insulting, ridiculous, and annoying, or perhaps both. Commercials in writing are fancy or unfamiliar words and terms or long-winded sentences that interrupt the reader's ability to follow or understand your message. For the most part, they need to be avoided. Even though you are often trying to "sell" an idea in daily business correspondence, why not let precise words and clearly expressed sentences do the "selling"?

In creating your first draft, construct short, simple sentences, with each expressing one idea. Later you can transform these sentences into longer or more detailed ones. The benefit of limiting each sentence to one idea will help you focus on the individual parts that need to be assembled into a cohesive whole. If you've ever built a model plane, ship, or car you know that first you have to assemble the various sections piece by piece before putting them all together. The same holds true for the sentences you construct.

Your first attempt might result in a rambling sentence such as this:

In order to make a manual as well-written as possible, a writer should, before he or she begins to write, consider the key steps or procedures essential for the user or operator to understand.

Upon second thought, you decide this revised version clearly states the focus:

When preparing a manual, the writer must consider the sequence of procedures.

Variety Is the Spice of Sentence Structure

Expressing your message initially by using simple sentences will help you focus on individual key details and concerns. Yet a series of simple sentences alone can result in a dull, choppy rhythm:

John is a competent manager. He often achieves his goals. He should be promoted.

Rather, these ideas can be combined to produce a more graceful flow of ideas:

. John, a competent manager who often achieves his goals, should be promoted.

Effective sentences are varied according to length and construction. All sentences need not begin with *the, a, an, it, there,* or *here* because the reader will soon weary of the monotonous repetition. The best sentences combine or interweave precise words and well-constructed phrases to create graceful, flowing rhythmic thought patterns.

Length

Sentences that average 10 to 20 words will convey your thoughts most effectively. Of course, shorter length alone is no guarantee of clarity. Still, sentences of 25 words or more have a greater tendency to confuse and disorient your reader or delay your message.

For example:

> I would appreciate it very much if each of you re-
> member that if there are any future occasions when it is
> necessary to bring matters like this regarding refunds to
> my attention to send your message to the Customer Ser-
> vice Department with a copy to me rather than sending
> the message directly to my attention. (55 words)

A sentence such as this contains quite a few "commer-
cials" that make the reader's journey longer than it needs to be.
If time is money, both writer and reader are paying too much.
Simply stated, the message could read:

> Please send all future messages regarding refunds di-
> rectly to Customer Service and forward a copy to me. (17
> words)

Sentence Structure

Combining short sentences into graceful ones is only one
of a number of helpful considerations you need to bear in mind
when constructing sentences. These techniques include:

Prefer Active to Passive Voice

Poor passive voice is so often maligned by writing instructors. Even grammar checkers consistently alert us to the
dangerous presence of a "passive construction." So what's so
bad about passive voice and just what is it? The truth is that
there's nothing wrong with passive voice. Rather, it's a question
of when and how to use it. Anyone trained in the technical
professions learned to appreciate the value and preference
for passive voice sentences to convey objectivity in reports,
tests, and other studies. The engineer learned to write "A problem
was found" rather than "I found a problem" to avoid using
the pronoun "I" and to convey information from a distance,
so to speak, that underscored the validity and objectivity of
his or her observations.

In active voice, the emphasis is placed on the subject or
doer of the action:

The manager wrote the report.

The active sentence is constructed according to basic English subject-verb-object sentence structure. Passive reverses the order and places the emphasis on the recipient of the action:

The report was written by the manager.

Both active and passive voice sentences are grammatically correct. It's a question of which one is most appropriate to the purpose and tone of your message.

Passive voice is best used when:

- You want the reader to focus on an activity or occurrence rather than who or what caused it to happen:
  Procedures have been written to ensure safety.

- The doer is unknown:
  The copy machine is broken.

- You don't want to assign blame:
  A mistake was made in processing the data.

- A process is described:
  The powder is added to the mixture.

Note: When writing instructions for the operator or user, always use active voice and place the verbs in the beginning of the sentence for emphasis:

Insert the card.

Do not write the weaker and less direct sentence:

The card is inserted.

I have often visualized active voice sentences as being similar to the quickest auto route, be it by highway, turnpike, or freeway. Passive voice, when appropriate or well constructed, is the scenic route. It takes a little longer to get there but it's worth it for the scenery, restaurants along the way, and historic sites. Poorly written or unnecessary passive voice represents the long way: construction, stop signs, traffic lights, railroad crossings, and so forth. You would never want to write (or read) this sentence:

> Your letter has been answered by me.

This is certainly passive voice at its worst. Remember that active voice sentences have greater vigor and often use fewer words to express your thoughts. When attempting to transform passive into active voice, ask yourself who or what is doing something and begin the sentence with the answer.

- PASSIVE: *The project was discussed by the supervisors.*
- ACTIVE: *The supervisors discussed the project.*

Expose Camouflaged Verbs

Verbs sometimes hide from your readers when introduced by other verbs such as *make, do, give, take, perform, provide, have,* and *be*:

> Martha will take under consideration the proposal.

The true verb (consider) is hidden by the helping verb and the sentence is longer than it should be:

> Martha will consider the proposal.

Shorten Prepositional Phrases

Your sentences may include phrases that begin with prepositions such as *in, for, to, on, with, above*, and others. One way to tighten the structure is to shorten these phrases to single words. Instead of writing:

> We are extending overtime in view of the fact that we need to complete several projects.

Try:

> We are extending overtime because we need to complete several projects.

Use Adjectives and Adverbs Instead of Phrases

You may recall that adjectives describe nouns (people, places, things) and adverbs describe or modify verbs. Whenever

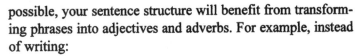
possible, your sentence structure will benefit from transforming phrases into adjectives and adverbs. For example, instead of writing:

> We have made reductions in the costs of our operation.

> Whenever there is a deadline, Victor writes in a quick way.

Try:

> We have reduced our operating (adjective) costs.

> Whenever there is a deadline, Victor writes quickly. (adverb)

Delete Unnecessary Articles, Prepositions, and Pronouns

Articles (a, an, the), prepositions (of), pronouns (it), and indicative words (there, here) can often be deleted from phrases and sentences where they serve little purpose. Instead of writing "many of the companies" or "the use of technology allows," try "many companies" and "technology allows." Rather than "It was our research department that provided the data," you could state, "Our research department provided the data."

You might ask what's so valuable about removing one or two brief words. The answer is that you achieve greater economy of expression even though nothing dramatic has been changed. Yet similar to the small monetary change you may toss daily into a jar, small changes in sentence structure can add up to improved flow of ideas.

Maintaining Balance and Importance: Coordinate and Subordinate Ideas

In our lives, we often understand the value of relationships, whether personal or professional. Sentences also contain elements or details that have relationships. It helps to be aware of opportunities for constructing sentences in which the ideas are *coordinated* (equal in importance or value) or *subordinated* (one idea is more important or dependent upon another for its meaning).

Sentence ideas can be coordinated by using connecting words and expressions such as *and, or, but, either...or,* and *neither...nor.*

Sentences Before Coordination:

The manager is seeking greater understanding of his assistant's concerns. The assistant wants the manager to understand her needs.

After Coordination:

The manager and his assistant seek better understanding of each other's needs.

Now the manager's and assistant's needs and expectations are expressed with greater balance and economy.

/ / /

Sentence elements can be subordinated by using words such as *after, when, while, if, since, although, through, before, until, whether, unless,* and *because* at the beginning or middle of a sentence.

Before Subordination:

Jack felt anxious about the interview. He knew he had a good chance of getting the job.

After Subordination:

Jack felt anxious about the interview although he knew he had a good chance of getting the job.

Subordinating Jack's belief in his ability to obtain the job to his anxiety underscores the prevalence or power of his nervousness.

Maintain Parallelism

Parallelism refers to a grammatical balance or structural consistency of various elements within your sentences. Sometimes the problem lies with the verb tenses or perhaps mixing active and passive voice in offering instructions or presenting a list that alternates between fragments and complete sentences. When you read a sentence lacking parallelism, you get the feeling that something is not quite right or that something impedes

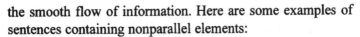
the smooth flow of information. Here are some examples of sentences containing nonparallel elements:

1. Derek has many hobbies. He likes to build model airplanes, racing vintage cars and collects arrowheads.
2. Paula is an intelligent, dedicated manager who is also cooperative.

In the first sentence the verbs are not consistent; in the second the adjective alone will suffice and needs to be placed before the noun it describes.

1. Derek has many hobbies. He likes to build model airplanes, race vintage cars and collect arrowheads.
2. Paula is an intelligent, dedicated and cooperative manager.

Don't Be Ambiguous

In our daily conversations, whenever we sense doubt or confusion in the listener's mind we can always explain our meaning. Usually we say, "In other words..." or "What I'm trying to say is..." or "Let me draw you a picture." In writing there's no opportunity to explain ourselves. Your readers either understand you or they don't. It's all or nothing, and the odds are against you, so you need to be aware of ambiguous sentences. The problem is that sometimes we don't see the possibility for confusion or interpretation because to us all is clear. So we may write:

The cost of the printer only was $100.

At first glance you may see little problem with this sentence. However, it can be interpreted in two ways: Are you saying that the printer alone, exclusive of all other equipment, cost $100 or that the price of the printer was $100? Whichever thought you want to express, the sentence must be rewritten to express either:

The printer cost only $100.

Or

The cost of only the printer was $100.

In speech, meaning is conveyed through the vocal emphasis we would place on the word *only* but in writing the reader can't hear the distinction. Even though the intended meaning of each sentence may be clear to us, we often have to ask ourselves if any sentence is prone to interpretation. If so, revise the sentence to remove that possibility. Sometimes the task may prove daunting, as in this sentence:

Jane told Barbara her handbag has been stolen.

Whose handbag was stolen? Can you really tell? When you suspect a sentence may be inclined to expressing a dual meaning, ask two people to read it and offer an opinion. If they differ or ask, "Is this what you're trying to say?" it's time to rewrite the sentence by beginning in your own mind with these words: "What I'm really trying to say here is...."

To Generalize Is to Err and Confuse

Generalizations are comparable to stereotypes. There may be some small truth inherent, but that is not enough to present the full picture. In fact, upon closer examination, we often discover that all stereotypes present distorted images of people and events. The success of your writing can be measured by your ability to progress from the general to the specific and from the abstract and vague to the concrete. Generalizations, such as those presented in this sentence, can only lead to confusion for your reader:

A majority of our customers preferred the new software.

Just how large was that majority? Fifty-three percent? Seventy-five percent? Ninety percent? Also, which new software do they prefer? The writer who sent this sentence to his manager no doubt received one back, asking these questions.

Fragments, Comma Splices, and Run-On Sentences Are No-Nos

In everyday conversations we often use fragment sentences to convey our thoughts. If someone in our office asks, "Where are you going?" we might answer, "To get coffee" or "Downstairs" or "Mary's office." In most instances, we have little trouble understanding fragmentary speech. Also, in speech we don't pronounce punctuation marks. Rather, our pauses or rhythms of expressions provide the commas and periods. When we're excited or in a rush our ideas are expressed through runaway sentences, long interconnected thoughts that often flow breathlessly. Writing, unfortunately, does not welcome any of these manners of communication. Writing, or rather your reader, insists upon complete thoughts.

You may ask, is that so? Then how is it that almost daily fragment sentences can be found in the most renowned newspapers and magazines? So why can't you do it? Well, you can. No one can truly stop you. After all, the use of fragments in those stories and articles is surely attributable to editorial or, in the writer's mind, poetic license.

Fiction writers may use fragments for atmospheric or realistic effect. In real life no one speaks in complete, perfectly constructed sentences. Still, you would be wise to avoid the following given the likelihood that your reader or reviewer does not feel inclined to granting you editorial or poetic license.

Fragment Sentence

Fragment sentences lack a subject, verb, or phrase to complete a thought.

Example:

A fine idea. (no subject or verb)

Correction:

Your suggestion is a fine idea.

Example:

Bob been promoted to supervisor. (Missing helping verb)

Correction:

Bob has been promoted to supervisor.

Example:

> While you were out.(missing phrase)

Correction:

> While you were out, your sister called.

Comma Splice Sentence

Comma splices occur when two independent complete sentences are joined by a comma and not followed by a conjunction (*and, or, but, for, so, nor, yet*) rather than a semicolon or separated by a period. (See *Appendix B* for Guidelines to Punctuation.)

Example:

> Alexis is busy writing a report this morning, after lunch, she can meet with you.

Corrections:

> Alexis is busy writing a report this morning, but after lunch, she is can meet with you.(Add a conjunction after the comma.)

> or

> Alexis is busy writing a report this morning; after lunch, she can meet with you.

(Place a semicolon between the sentences.)

> or

> Alexis is busy writing a report this morning. After lunch, she can meet with you.

(Place a period between the sentences.)

Run-On Sentence

Run-on sentences lack any punctuation and are among the most troublesome of all, because your reader has no idea where ideas begin and end.

Example:

> We have decided that our policies and procedures are confusing therefore we have decided to revise them we

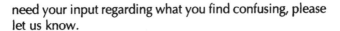
need your input regarding what you find confusing, please let us know.

Correction:

We have decided that our policies and procedures are confusing. Therefore, we have decided to revise them. We need your input regarding what you find confusing. Please let us know.

Sentence Structure

The best sentences combine simplicity of expression with a certain amount of sophistication. Here are some pitfalls to avoid:

The Overuse of the Word *and* to Connect Too Many Independent Sentences

Either place periods between the sentences or rewrite them to condense the information.

Example:

Judy is a very fine organizer and she has a very good sense of time management and her ability to relate to people is a definite talent and I believe she is the person who will best represent our organization at the conference next month.

Revision:

Judy is a very fine organizer with a very good sense of time management. Because her ability to relate to people is a definite talent, I believe she is the person who will best represent our organization at the conference next month.

Double Negatives to Prevent Confusing Your Readers

Example:

It is not unwise of Sandy to decide not to change the supervisor's observations.

Ordering the new software is not unnecessary.

Revision:

Sandy is wise to avoid challenging the supervisor's observations.

Ordering the new software is necessary.

Separating Related Parts of Compound Verbs

Example:

Charlie decided, even though Connie objected, to go bowling instead of to the opera.

Revision:

Even though Connie objected, Charlie decided to go to bowling instead of to the opera.

Dangling Participles (Beginning a Sentence With an "-ing" Phrase Unrelated to the Words That Follow

Example:

Drinking a cup of tea, the doorbell rang.

Revision:

I was drinking a cup of tea when the doorbell rang.

Sentences Beginning With Infinitive Phrases (to Play, to Write, and So on) That Result in Awkward Structure and Confusion

Example:

To return the package quickly, a small fee was charged.

Revision:

The shipper charged a small fee to return the package quickly.

High-Strung Sentences

Just as high-strung people can be difficult to get along with, so can sentences that contain too many descriptive words strung together in uninterrupted sequence. For example:

> The manual explains Distribution Center management personnel training.

> We have decided to use a training needs planning summary survey.

Sentences with these strung-together words challenge your reader to untangle the words and sort them into a coherent order by way of intellectual cut-and-paste work. By using connective articles, prepositions, and pronouns, the revised sentences will read:

> The manual explains training of management personnel in the Distribution Center.

> We have decided to use a survey to plan and summarize our training needs.

Which sentences would you rather receive?

Building Blocks of Ideas: Paragraphs

If words are the tools that "build" sentences, paragraphs help to arrange your ideas into "building blocks" of information. Paragraphs, often defined as individual units or sections of thought, help you expand and develop your ideas.

Introductory Paragraphs

Good introductory paragraphs state your main idea, focus, purpose, or need. Introductory paragraphs are similar to first impressions. Keep in mind that if you don't get the reader's attention in the beginning, you may not get it at all. When we read a book, attend a movie, or turn on the television or radio, consider how important the beginning is, whether the first pages or the first few minutes of the film or program or broadcast. If we don't find what we see or hear interesting, we place the book aside, ask for a refund at the theater, or change the channel or station.

You don't want your reader to change channels when it comes to your writing.

Example

The purpose of this series of workshops is to provide you with the concepts and theories to develop marketing and management strategies for selected markets for our products and services. Although these markets have their particular requirements, in general, a clearly articulated and focused marketing strategy is required to serve these markets effectively and profitably.

Supporting Paragraphs

The opening paragraph is followed by supporting details or data that elaborate on your initial point of interest or central idea.These consist of examples, figures, numerical data, dates, observations, file numbers—anything that expands, explains, or offers support to your message. The ideas must flow smoothly from the opening to middle to concluding paragraphs. Sentences and paragraphs have relationships that must be indicated.

Example

Marketing is defined as detecting and meeting customer needs at a profit. As you develop a marketing strategy, it is important to think in terms of what our unique products and services can offer. If your marketing efforts are to be successful, they must address the needs of the buyer. For this reason, the market planning and management processes that you will be learning in these workshops will focus on ways to help you develop a marketing strategy that emphasizes accurate assessment of the customer's needs. For this series of workshops, you will be divided into several work groups, each of which will

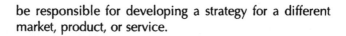

be responsible for developing a strategy for a different market, product, or service.

Directional Words: The Highway Signs of Writing

Imagine traveling cross country by car along a highway with many entrance and exit ramps but no signs. How would you know where to get off? The same applies to paragraph structure: You need to provide directions to your reader that advise of where some ideas begin, round a curve, proceed up-hill, change direction, or end. The following list of transition or directional words and phrases can serve as the highway signs to your writing. They will help you initiate your thoughts and provide transitions and continuity among sentences within a paragraph or among the paragraphs themselves.

To Indicate Comparison, Reversal, or Limitation:

- but.
- however.
- nevertheless.
- on the contrary.
- on the other hand.
- conversely.
- yet.
- although.
- even though.

Examples:

Michael wants to attend an opera, but Margo prefers to see a Broadway comedy.

Dave is, on the other hand, a superb manager.

To Indicate Addition and Continuity:

- and.
- also.
- moreover.

- in addition.
- in the same manner.
- furthermore.
- likewise.
- similarly.

Examples:

Vinny is a musician and his brother is a lawyer.

We are, in addition, planning to buy a house in the country.

To Indicate Time Order or Sequence:

- first.
- next.
- beforeafter.
- subsequently.
- consequently.
- concurrently.
- currently.
- later.
- soon.
- immediately.
- then.
- last.

Example:

Before you begin writing the report, first you need to establish your purpose, then consider your reader, and last decide upon the central focus of your study.

To Indicate Instance or Example:

- for example.
- for instance.
- in particular.
- in general.

Example:

The film Jeremy directed recently, for example, clearly shows his talent for comedy.

To Indicate Emphasis:

- in fact.
- primarily.
- significantly.
- most important.
- indeed.
- certainly.
- undoubtedly.

Example:

Pamela has, in fact, already expressed her support for the new program.

To Indicate Conclusion or Consequence:

- finally.
- in conclusion.
- as a result.
- eventually.
- so.
- therefore.
- in summary.
- in closing.

Example:

We are, therefore, confident the new procedures will lead to improved customer service.

And So: Concluding Paragraphs

The closing sentence completes the thought or serves as a transition to the next paragraph.

Example

>   At the end of the last workshop on Friday, each group will present a summary and visual presentation of its strategy to the other groups and senior management. In addition, after the training program each group will be responsible for preparing a written presentation for senior managers interested in the various workshop topics.

Paragraph Length

Writing quality is difficult to quantify and so too are the lengths for paragraphs. Some editors suggest five to seven sentences; others suggest no more than 100 words; still others believe a fifth or quarter of a page is a sensible limit. Another theory is to measure your paragraphs to see if they exceed two inches. There's no one best way. Just remember that in general paragraphs need to begin with a sentence that conveys a main idea or important detail or element of your message.

Example of a Developing Paragraph

First Version

>   Coronado & Company is a leading nationwide provider of diagnostic imaging services and operator of state-of-the-art mobile diagnostic imaging systems and related outsourced radiology services in the United States.

This paragraph offers a fairly straightforward description of the company's services. The reader is provided with general information about the company and no more.

Second Version

>   Coronado & Company is a leading nationwide provider of diagnostic imaging services and operator of state-of-the-art mobile diagnostic imaging systems and related outsourced radiology services in the United States. The company primarily provides MRI systems and services as well as full-service management of imaging operations.

This version adds descriptive information that provides the reader with specific details about the equipment and services, therefore extending the range of the initial opening statement.

Third Version

Coronado & Company is a leading mobile MRI (magnetic resonance imaging) service provider in the United States. The company primarily provides MRI systems and services to hospitals on a mobile share basis and operates MRI fixed site units on hospital campuses. Coronado & Company's services allow hospitals to gain access to advanced diagnostic imaging technology and valuable technical support services without having to invest in equipment and personnel.

This version offers a more comprehensive view of the company. The opening now includes a definition of the acronym MRI and a closing sentence expressing the financial and staffing benefits the company's services offer to hospitals.

Paragraphs: Divide and Conquer

Uninterrupted blocks of information can easily overwhelm your reader. Always look for opportunities to divide the information into segments or components. Smaller pieces of information are often easier to digest and allow your reader to more readily absorb the information. For example:

GSP Wireless, Inc. is the largest provider of mobile phone equipment and services in the South. The company has a strong presence in all of the southeastern and western states from North Carolina to Florida to Arizona. Currently, GSP Wireless enjoys a 5-percent market share and is expected to increase with future acquisition of smaller, lesser-known competitors. GSP Wireless has a strong name recognition and reputation for quality equipment and exceptional service. The company is the largest operator of state-of-the-art wireless phone equipment and services compared to its competitors. GSP Wireless has substantial financial flexibility and access to lower-cost capital to expand its market base, engage in product research and development, and offer service plans to meet a wide range of customer needs and budgets.

Although the passage is generally readable, the amount of details combined with its length results in information overload for the reader. Dividing this passage into smaller paragraphs produces a more accessible format:

> GSP Wireless, Inc. is the largest provider of mobile phone equipment and services in the South. The company has a strong presence in all of the southeastern and western states from North Carolina to Florida to Arizona. Currently GSP Wireless enjoys a 51-percent market share, which is expected to increase with future acquisition of smaller, lesser-known competitors.
>
> GSP Wireless has a strong name recognition and reputation for quality equipment and exceptional service. The company is the largest operator of state-of-the-art wireless phone equipment and services compared to its competitors.
>
> GSP Wireless has substantial financial flexibility and strength due to surplus cash flow and access to lower-cost capital to expand its market base, engage in product research and development, and offer numerous service plans to meet a wide range of customer needs and budgets.

Play the Numbers Game

Whenever a paragraph contains a list or sequence, you can highlight that order of information for your reader simply by changing the structure of the paragraph from a series of sentences to a numbered list of phrases, sentences, or smaller paragraphs. For example, if you were describing the investment merits of a company to potential investors, your first draft may present the information in this manner:

Investment Merits

> These following aspects allow Good Fun Industries considerable advantages over its competitors. Acquisitions

have played a significant role in the Good Fun Industries' growth strategy, emphasized by a recent agreement to acquire LPN Foods for $45 million, which will increase sales volume. Good Fun is capitalizing on its leading position by seeking growth through acquisitions, by offering international food products, thus extending its customer base. The company is reducing costs by obtaining higher purchasing discounts and consolidating warehouse facilities. Good Fun's market share is 43 percent, which is approximately the size of its two next competitors combined. Other

10 Guidelines to Construct Better Paragraphs

Well-constructed paragraphs result in easier reading for your readers. Paragraphs help your readers "digest" larger masses of information that otherwise might be overwhelming in complexity of thought, amount of supporting details, or length. Here are 10 guidelines to constructing effective paragraphs:

1. Focus on one main idea in each paragraph.
2. State the topic or focus of each paragraph in the opening sentence.
3. Include only relevant or illustrative supporting details.
4. Prefer shorter (3–7 sentences, 100–125 words) to longer paragraphs (one-half page or more).
5. Vary the length of paragraphs within each page or document.
6. Use linking words or phrases (*however, for example, therefore, next, most important*) to ensure a smooth transition among sentences and paragraphs.
7. Repeat key words and ideas to enhance emphasis and importance to your readers.
8. Use various patterns of thinking and writing such as *problem/solution, cause/effect, comparison/contrast, time order* to convey logical organization of ideas.
9. Present ideas in terms of individual "building blocks" of information.
10. Use numbers or letters within parentheses before sentences in paragraphs that list information in sequence.

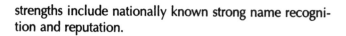

strengths include nationally known strong name recognition and reputation.

Revised Version

The following aspects allow Good Fun Industries considerable advantages over its competitors:

1. Acquisitions have played a significant role in the Good Fun Industries' growth strategy, emphasized by a recent agreement to acquire LPN Foods for $45 million, which will increase sales volume.
2. Good Fun is capitalizing in its leading position by seeking growth through acquisitions, by offering international food products, thus extending its customer base.
3. The company is reducing costs by obtaining higher purchasing discounts and consolidating warehouse facilities.
4. Good Fun's market share is 43 percent, which is approximately the size of its two next competitors combined.
5. Other strengths include nationally known strong name recognition and reputation.

Who Do You Think You Are?
Tone and Style

"Style is the dress of thoughts."
—Lord Chesterfield

*"Proper words in proper places
make the true definition of style."*
—Jonathan Swift

*"When we come across a natural style, we are
surprised and delighted; for we expected
an author, and we find a man."*
—Blaise Pascal

HOW OFTEN HAVE YOU OVERHEARD someone complain, "It's not what he said but how he said it. Who does he think he's talking to?" Tone of voice is an important factor in our professional and personal relationships. When you neglect to use the appropriate tone in speech or writing, you undermine your reader's ability to respond with a positive or open attitude to your message, no matter how important or logical or persuasive its content. In the sets of sentences that follow, notice how your response to each sentence differs according to its tone of voice.

   1a.   We feel no further obligation to assist in this matter.
   1b.   We have provided all the help we can regarding this matter.

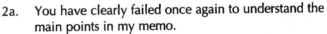

2a.   You have clearly failed once again to understand the main points in my memo.

2b.   I need to explain several key points in my memo.

3a.   We told you and we repeat we have no interest in your invention.

3b.   Thank you for offering to sell us your invention. Unfortunately, the benefits it provides lie outside our daily production needs.

Unless you're a mean-spirited person, most likely you appreciate the second sentence in each set due to its less negative, and hence, more professional tone. The first sentences indicate stubborn noncompliance to a request, dissatisfaction, annoyance, and irritation, not the most welcoming of feelings directed to the reader. You will find that generally people will respond positively to incoming writing even when they are feeling stressed or angry, provided the message is not openly hostile or confrontational. The "partly sunny" day is always more inviting than the "partly cloudy" one.

It's all a question of attitude. Telemarketers advise their staffs to keep a mirror in front of their phones and to smile into it before dialing potential customers. The theory is that the listener can hear more from the tone of your voice than the words. If you forgot to sign a credit-card application, you would most likely rather learn that "We need your signature in order to process this application." rather than "You failed to sign the application."

Feelings

Emotions can easily intrude upon the most simple messages. Some people can send us letters and e-mail messages that are clearly hostile or nasty and tempt us to respond in kind. At times maybe we should. How would you feel if you received this message?

Whose job do you think you can do better? Mine or yours?

Most likely you'd feel like socking the person who sent it. There are certainly people who can push us over the edge of civilized decorum. The question is how to respond to them. In this case, perhaps it's best not to respond at all. The writer is clearly upset and resentful, perhaps even insecure about something you may have said or suggested. If you receive an unsettling message such as this, do not respond immediately. No matter how justified or outraged you feel, your emotions will get the better of your ability to express your thoughts and, ironically enough, you may end up appearing the aggressor. Perhaps one way to ensure an appropriate tone is to follow the advice of 19th-century English novelist Anthony Trollope, who suggested that there "should be a rule through the letter writing world: that no angry letter be posted till four-and-twenty hours will have elapsed." Here are additional guidelines:

1. **Consider** your relationship with the reader. Familiar? Formal? Tense? Friendly? Business?

2. **Identify** the reader's likely point of view, needs, expectations, concerns, possible prejudices, attitudes, and interests.

3. **Determine** the purpose of your message. Is there more than one purpose?

4. **Understand** how much detail the reader will need (for example, times, dates, names, addresses, telephone, e-mail, fax numbers, or examples) to avoid his or her experiencing frustration, annoyance, or information overload.

5. **Ask** yourself how much the reader may be interested in the content. What function or value can the message provide in terms of interests, benefits, decision-making, and/or understanding of problems, procedures, or incidents?

6. **Avoid** a pompous or arrogant tone. In comedy, audiences always appreciate seeing the pompous or arrogant knave slip on that banana peel or receive a whipped-cream pie in the face. Self-importance in

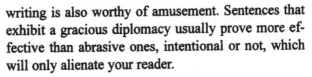

writing is also worthy of amusement. Sentences that exhibit a gracious diplomacy usually prove more effective than abrasive ones, intentional or not, which will only alienate your reader.

Instead of:

In the future see to it that this office does not have to remind you to submit your expense vouchers on time.

Write:

Please remember you must submit your expense vouchers on time.

7. **Avoid** seeming indifferent. Indifference is worse than anger or refusal. For writers, artists, composers, and filmmakers a poor review is usually better than no review. Seeming indifference will never earn your reader's good graces.

Instead of:

The responsibility for reviewing proposals clearly belongs to our Purchasing Department. This department is interested only in matters concerning safety.

Write:

The Purchasing Department is responsible for reviewing proposals. Our department is limited to administering safety programs.

8. **Avoid** being offensive or outright insulting. No one appreciates rudeness or being insulted. Even when understood to be in jest, feelings often get rattled or egos can receive a bruising not likely to be soon forgotten.

Never write:

Obviously, your thinking on this issue is so far-fetched and in the twilight zone of incredible absurdity that only a half-wit could understand what you are trying to say.

Instead:

There are some points in your comments (underlined) I would appreciate your clarifying.

Writing Negative Messages to Managers and Executives

When you have to write a negative message upwards to your manager, the vice president, the CEO, or perhaps the board of directors of your company, you naturally feel a considerable degree of anxiety, and no wonder. After all, you want to impress these important readers. You want to be perceived as being intelligent, professional, hardworking, efficient, and highly skillful in conveying your thoughts in writing.

Your reader, on the other hand, is simply interested in obtaining a clear understanding of your main message. How often have you heard these high level readers say: "Just tell me what I need to know in a few sentences or a short paragraph." In other words, don't waste my time; it's too valuable. You, of course, hope beyond hope that you will not become the proverbial victim of the bearer of bad news. So here's one method for communicating negative tidings and not suffering the wrath of the gods of industry.

1. First, consider your relationship to the reader. Do you have frequent communication or interaction with this individual? Is he or she friendly towards you or at least respectful? How about personality traits or corporate image? Nice? Pompous? Cold? Reserved? Formal? Cheerful? Easy-going? Always stressed? Rude? Overbearing? Impatient? Calm?

2. The more you know or think you know about this higher-level reader, the more confident you may feel in writing to him or her. In any case, use a pleasant or neutral opening sentence. Do not just blurt out the bad news. Proceed with caution, but do proceed.

3. Explain the reasons or provide brief background details surrounding the bad news.

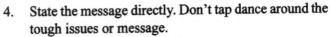
4. State the message directly. Don't tap dance around the tough issues or message.

5. Then, if possible, suggest optimism for future resolution of the negative issue and close cordially.

Example

TO: Sam Fischer
FROM: George Woodruff
DATE: April 30
SUBJECT: Status of West Palm Research & Development Center

As requested, I have evaluated the current status of construction of the West Palm Research & Development Center. Unusually strong winds and heavy rains resulted in extensive delays in suppliers' ability to deliver essential materials. As a result, there is only minimal progress to report. The current mild sunny weather and temperature, however, are expected to continue throughout May, during which time considerable progress is expected.

Sunny, Blue-Skies Words

Words have denotative (dictionary) meanings and connotative (suggestive) ones. What often matters in ensuring that your writing conveys a tone appropriate to your purpose is the feeling a particular word invokes in your reader. Advertisers know the value of promising their products and services will offer trouble-free operation or solve your problems or guarantee peace of mind. No computer is ever advertised as slower than the previous model, nor is software touted as nearly impossible for the average person to understand. Hardly. So here is a list of words that will more often than not evoke in your reader's mind sunny days, blue skies, and soft sandy beaches lined with palm trees or any other pleasant image:

ability	cooperation	exceptional	kind
advantage	courtesy	exclusive	lasting
approval	dependable	genuine	merit
attractiveness	desirable	good	notable
benefit	distinction	guarantee	opportunity
beneficial	diversity	helpful	popular
capable	ease	honest	practical
comfort	economy	humor	prominent
commendable	effective	improvement	reliable
comprehensive	efficient	initiative	responsible
confidence	enthusiasm	integrity	satisfaction
convenience	excellence	intelligence	value

Stormy-Weather Words

Just as all days do not have to be sunny, so too does tone not have to be always positive. There are times when you will need to write a negative memo or e-mail; letter of complaint; poor evaluation of an employee, product, or service; or response to unjustified criticism. Then you will want to use the list that follows. (Just remember that when you use these words, you should do so intentionally.)

alleged	erroneous	meager
blame	exaggerate	mediocre
careless	extravagant	misfortune
cheap	fail	neglectful
collusion	failure	negligence
commonplace	fault	obstinate
deadlock	fiasco	opinionated
discredit	flagrant	oversight
disgusting	implicate	premature
disreputable	impossible	rude
disrupt	insolvent	squander
embarrassing	irritation	superficial

The Tone Is You

Writers of fiction strive to find a truthful balance between life as it is lived and as it is imagined. Tone demands a balancing act of words as well. Just remember that whatever you write will have your name on it. People who have never met or spoken with you will learn quite a bit about you simply from the tone of your voice and words.

8

Last Restroom for 300 Miles: Editing for Content and Structure

"Read over a passage, and wherever you meet a passage which you think is particularly fine, cross it out."
—Samuel Johnson

"Not that the story need be long, but it will take a long while to make it short."
—Henry David Thoreau

"I believe more in the scissors than I do in the pencil."
—Truman Capote

IMAGINE THIS SCENARIO: YOU ARE driving out West and about to travel through miles of desert. At the edge of the desert, you come upon a gas station and notice a large sign that announces "Last Gas Station for 300 Miles." Would you stop? Most people would. It makes sense to check out the gas, tire pressure, water coolant level, oil, and whatnot and maybe use the restroom. Yet there is always that one driver who doesn't feel the need to bother and simply drives straight into the desert. Most likely we will see that car again along the way, hood up and steam pouring out of the engine or just plain out of gas. The same lesson applies to editing your writing. If you don't believe you need to edit for content and structure, you are more than likely to regret it.

Cold Eyes: The Key to Editing

Some years ago a man attending one of my writing seminars expressed a somewhat poetic view of editing I have always remembered. He said the challenge when editing is to "look upon the writing with cold eyes." The image of coldness so aptly conveys the objective distance all writers need to achieve when editing first and subsequent drafts. We all need to establish a distance between ourselves and our initial writing. Of course, the difficulty lies in our tendency to believe everything we write to be clearly expressed simply because we always understand it or know what we want to say. No wonder we're shocked and annoyed when the reader advises us to explain ourselves a bit further. So we need to achieve some space between what is subjective (the writing) but needs to be viewed objectively (editing).

Editing requires time and patience. Most of us are in a hurry to be rid of e-mail, memos, letters, reports, and other assignments and move on to the next task. Moreover, a lot of writers confuse editing with proofreading. Although the two often overlap, proofreading is directed primarily towards reviewing for mechanical correctness (spelling, grammar, punctuation, capitalization, usage), whereas editing focuses on reviewing for clarity of content, format, tone, and logical organization of ideas. Although separate in focus and goals, editing and proofreading are activities designed to improve the quality of your writing. As the novelist E. M. Forster once observed: "How do I know what I think until I see what I say?"

Slow Down

Ideally, we would write in the morning and edit in the afternoon. Such an approach would enhance our ability to view our work objectively. The distance in time alone would provide us with the objectivity so essential to effective editing. Yet we don't always have the luxury of time to provide a helpful distance between the first draft and final version. Much of what we write needs to be transmitted without delay to our readers or reviewers. It would seem that time and tide and the need to distribute the writing wait for none of us. The special urgency or expectation for a quick or immediate response to incoming e-mail compounds the tendency to dash off our first thoughts to the impatient reader in cyberspace.

Edit Accordingly

You may now be wondering how many times a document has to be edited to ensure its effectiveness. There is no one answer to this question except to bear in mind that everything we write does not need to be edited any given number of times or in the same way. The amount of time spent editing depends on the complexity of the content and your relationship with your reader. For instance, a simple e-mail or memo distributed within your department would probably benefit from editing once. Letters, faxes, and instructions should be edited twice; reports, contracts, manuals, proposals, documentation, and other more formal writing could use at least three edits. If you are working on an ongoing assignment such as a manual that requires continued addition and deletion of information, then you must go beyond three edits. The danger in over-editing lies in the likelihood you will face the dilemma of trying to determine this: "Did I make it better or merely different?" Always allow some time, even a minute or two, between your first draft message and efforts to revise and polish it. Print a copy of that e-mail message before sending it. Review the letter one more time before sending it.

Content or Style?

During my writing seminars, I am often asked: "Why is it that when my boss edits my work, she sees a lot of mistakes I didn't see even though I read the document five times?" The answer is simple: The reviewer didn't write it. Asking another person for an opinion of your writing can be helpful because your reviewer will have a natural distance from the work. At the same time, this individual may not have your technical expertise or fully understand the circumstances surrounding your goals or reasons for writing. Worse, the comments, suggestions, and observations might reflect opinions, personal style,

 ## Editorial Checklist

1. Did I provide a main idea or topic sentence to inform the reader of my purpose and focus?
2. Have I supplied all essential details to support my statement?
3. Is the information presented in order of importance?
4. Does the organization suit the reader's needs? For example, should I provide a summary?
5. Does each sentence and paragraph contribute to the general flow of ideas?
6. Are the sentences and paragraphs presented in a logical order?
7. Does each paragraph fully develop its topic?
8. Did I supply directional or linking words to connect sentences and paragraphs?
9. Is the language level suited to the reader?
10. Has unnecessary technical jargon been eliminated?
11. Are all sentences expressed clearly, precisely, and economically?
12. Did I prefer active to passive voice wherever possible?
13. Is the tone appropriate?
14. Is there any unnecessary repetition of ideas?
15. Are there gaps or missing material that may cause the reader confusion?
16. Are there ambiguous sentences or phrases that may be misunderstood or misinterpreted?
17. Are there any digressions?
18. Is there any extraneous information that should be placed in an appendix or not included?
19. Did I proofread for spelling, grammar, punctuation, and usage?

and other editorial preferences. Whatever the advice or suggestions you receive, it will often remain your decision to incorporate them in your work.

Revise the Beginning, Middle, and End

Another complaint I hear from those attending my seminars is this: "When I try to edit my work I really don't know what to look for." The editorial checklist on page 102 is designed to help you answer this question. Be sure to add to this list your own reminders and questions regarding your personal editorial needs, such as checking for correct use of commas or complex verb endings or avoiding fragments. Modify this list for your own purposes.

The majority of business writing, ranging from e-mail, memos, and letters to reports, instructions, and proposals, is likely to have a beginning, middle, and end. Each section serves a distinct purpose:

1. To introduce your message (opening).
2. To provide supporting details (middle).
3. To present concluding remarks (conclusion).

Because everything we write can benefit from revision, whether minimal or extensive, the following guidelines will help you to ensure the effectiveness of each section.

The Opening

When revising your opening statement, ensure that it states your purpose and topic clearly and, if possible, in a manner to arouse your reader's interest. You may want to begin with a statement of fact. For example:

> Recent reports show that durable goods orders rose in June for the third month out of four, claims for unemployment are lower this year than the during the same quarter of last year, and retail rates sales are rising.

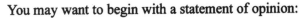

You may want to begin with a statement of opinion:

I'm certain that stocks and bonds prices will rise substantially in response to this morning's government announcement regarding economic growth expectations.

The Body

When revising the body of discussion, remember that each sentence must contribute to developing your message. Eliminate excess baggage of words, so to speak. One helpful technique is to imagine you are being charged by the word.

The Conclusion

When revising the conclusion or closing you can restate the main point, summarize main ideas, draw a conclusion, suggest a recommendation based upon previously provided details, or urge action. For example:

As a result of the changes in our production schedule, we must hire additional personnel immediately.

Examples of Convoluted Writing

The following examples of business writing may lead to undue stress for the reader as a result of confusion, frustration, or anger with the writer.

From an Insurance Company Booklet:

You are not insured under one paragraph of a Clause or under one Clause for any risk insurable under another paragraph of that Clause or under another Clause or for any risk which is not insured by reason of any exclusion, qualification, additional term or condition applicable to such other paragraph or Clause or because you are not insured under such other paragraph or Clause.

And don't forget it! Although you might agree that the previous paragraph is impossible for the average person to understand, you might also suggest it's unfair to criticize this passage because it is simply (?) reflecting the necessary legal language of insurance policies. Yet, if the policy is written for the average person, should it sound like that? Isn't there another way to express the details and maintain the necessary legal implications without causing stress? I showed this passage to several insurance industry professionals and all agreed the language was dense. Most admitted they had to read the passage three or more times to understand it, and even afterwards could only attempt to "interpret" the true meaning, which remains a secret to all but the writer.

From a Corporate Prospectus:

Each note will bear interest from its date of issue at the fixed rate per annum or at the rate per annum determined pursuant to the interest rate formula, stated therein and in the applicable pricing supplement, until the principal thereof is paid or made available for payment. The applicable pricing supplement relating to a fixed rate note will designate a fixed rate of interest per annum payable on such note. Unless otherwise indicated in the applicable Pricing Supplement, each note will be paid semi-annually each June 1 and December 1 and at stated maturity or, if applicable, upon redemption. If any interest payment date or the stated maturity date (or, if applicable, the date of redemption) of a fixed rate note falls on a day that is not a business day, payment of principal, premium, if any, or interest will be made on the next business day as if were made on the date such payment was due, and no interest will accrue on the amount so payable for the period from and after such interest payment date or the stated maturity (or the date of redemption), as the case may be. The record dates for such notes will be the May 15 and November 15 next preceding the June 1 and December 1 interest payment dates.

Unless otherwise indicated in the applicable pricing supplement, interest payments for fixed rate notes shall be the amount of interest accrued to, but excluding, the relevant interest payment date. Interest on such notes will be computed on the basis of a 360-day year of 12 30-day months.

Now take a few minutes to catch your breath or allow the dizziness to pass! This passage suffers not just the barrage of redundant legalese but from the following:

1. Lengthy paragraph structure.
2. Absence of subheadings to allow the reader to pause to process each important idea.
3. Failure to provide definitions of financial terms.
4. Excessively long sentences (some more than 75 words).

Here is a revised version that's easier on your nerves:

Annual Interest Rate

The yearly interest rate on the notes will either be fixed or floating. The applicable pricing supplement will designate the fixed rate of interest payable on a note. Interest will be paid on June 1 and December 1, and upon maturity, redemption, or repurchase.

Payment and Record Dates

If any payment date falls on a day that is not a business day, payment will be made on the next business day but no additional interest will be paid. The record dates for such notes will be May 15 (for interest to be paid on June 1) and November 15 (for interest to be paid on December 1).

Computation of Interest Payments

Interest payments will be the amount of interest accrued to but excluding each June 1 and December 1. Interest will be computed using a 360-day year of 12 30-day months.

Which version would you rather receive? Sometimes the solution is simply to transform a block of information into a series of lists. For example, consider the following:

Floating Rate Notes: The applicable pricing supplement relating to a floating rate note will designate an interest rate formula for such floating rate note. Such a formula may be the commercial paper rate, in which case such note will be a commercial paper rate; the prime rate, in which case such note will be a prime rate note; the CD rate, in which case such note will be a CD rate note; the federal funds effective rate, in which case such note will be a federal funds effective rate; the Treasury rate, in which case such note will be a Treasury rate note; such other interest rate formula as is set forth in such pricing supplement. The applicable pricing supplement for a floating rate note also will specify the spread and/or spread multiplier, if any, applicable to each note. Any floating rate note may also have either or both of the following: a maximum numerical interest rate limitation, or ceiling or a minimum numerical interest rate limitation, or floor.

Now consider this revised version, in which the information is presented in list format:

Floating Rate Notes

Each floating rate note will have an interest rate formula, which may be based on the:

- Commercial paper rate.
- Prime rate.
- CD rate.
- Federal funds effective rate.
- Treasury rate.
- Another interest rate.

The applicable pricing supplement will also indicate any spread and/or spread multiplier. In addition, any floating rate note may have a maximum or minimum interest rate limitation.

Avoid Sexist Wording

The world of work has changed considerably over the last 25 years. Women have moved far beyond the limitations of secretarial or clerical duties and hold important professional, administrative, and technical positions few of their grandmothers ever hoped to achieve. Correspondence traditionally addressed to "Gentlemen" or "Dear Sirs" is considered archaic by modern standards. Also, what woman would tolerate her male manager referring to her as "my girl," no matter how innocent the intention? Jobs titles reflect these changes: mail carriers, police officers, and flight attendants are some examples. Some actresses prefer to be known as actors and the words *poetess* and *authoress* have gone the way of the manual typewriter. Waiters and waitresses are now gender-neutral "servers." For these reasons, be careful to check your writing for remarks or references that may appear sexist or offensive.

You can revise your sentences to eliminate the masculine pronoun by:

Repeating the Noun

When a manager approves a proposal, the manager....

Using Plural Nouns and Pronouns

When engineers review plans, they....

Using "He" or "She"

If a customer wants to return the product, he or she....

Using Passive Voice

When a student uses our service, the student is assured....

Editorial Hit List: Little Things Mean a Lot

The Best Word Wins

There really is no best word; rather, there is a simpler one or more familiar one or less convoluted or technical one or specific or more appropriate one. Word choice is best determined according to your purpose, relationship with the reader, and appropriate tone, and not the number of syllables or impressive sound. The best helpful guide is a dictionary of synonyms, which will help you expand the range of your word "toolbox" and provide you with a Phillips head screwdriver when a flathead one won't do.

1. Simpler or shorter word

- *try* for *attempt.*
- *part* for *component.*
- *similar* for *analogous.*

2. Familiar word

- *payment* for *remuneration.*
- *postpone* for *abeyance.*
- *confuse* for *obfuscate.*

3. Non-technical word

- *two million pieces of data* for *two megabytes.*

4. Specific word

- *research center* for *facility.*

5. Excessive nouns, verbs, and articles

- *biochemistry* for *the field of biochemistry.*
- *investigations* for *the conducting of investigations.*
- *experimentation* for *the process of experimentation.*
- *look* for *take a look at.*
- *decide* for *make a decision.*
- *many managers* for *many of the managers.*
- *several reports* for *several of the reports.*

6. Words That Shouldn't Be Married

- managerwise.
- reportwide.
- strategize.

7. Words That Say It Twice

- green in color.
- round in shape.
- but however.

- and also.
- finally in conclusion.

8. Latin or Foreign Language Words

- quid pro quo.
- cul de sac.
- zeitgeist.
- au contraire.
- non de plume.

9. Familiar but Overused Nonstandard Words and Phrases

- impact (as a verb).
- cutting edge.

10. Optional Use of "who, whom, that, which"

- The nurse whom I met last night in Atlanta.
- A city that I love to visit.
- The car which was parked illegally was towed.

Options:

- The nurse I met last night in Atlanta...
- A city I love to visit...
- The car parked illegally was towed...

Problems With Sentence Structure

Here are the most common problems regarding sentence structure:

Shift in Verb Tense

Example:

While we were in the restaurant snow is beginning to fall.

Revision:

While we were in the restaurant, snow began to fall.

The original sentence begins with the past tense and then shifts to present tense even though both actions occur at the same time.

Shift in Point of View

Example:

Before anyone sends an e-mail, you should always proofread it.

Revision:

Before anyone sends an e-mail, he or she should always proofread it.

The shift from the singular pronoun to second person is inconsistent.

Shift in Focus

Example:

When you visit Venice, an overwhelming sense of the past is experienced.

Revision:

When visiting Venice, you experience an overwhelming sense of the past.

Word Omission

Example:

I was listening to music and my girlfriend typing her novel.

Revision:

I was listening to music and my girlfriend was typing her novel.

Omission of even seemingly unimportant words can result in awkwardness and cause confusion.

Repetitive Subjects

Example:

The customer, she gave me a dirty look.

Revision:

The customer gave me a dirty look.

Although we often repeat words to reinforce their importance to our reader, sometimes repetition of the subject only results in redundancy.

Writing for Another Person's Approval or Signature

"No passion in the world is equal to the passion to alter someone else's draft."

—H. G. Wells

Writing for another person's approval or signature almost requires your being able to read someone else's mind. How many times have you been asked by your boss to write a memo or letter, only to learn when you submit it that "it's not what I want to say"? So you write it again, present the revised version and hear, "No. That's still not what I want to say." Exasperating? Of course it is, but getting approval from another person is an unavoidable aspect of writing within any size corporate hierarchy of power. No one is ever free of criticism.

For some supervisors it will never be good enough. Sometimes these people have very high standards, and that's fine, but they are unable to see that everyday business writing cannot always be flawless. These people are often perfectionists or are so concerned about their corporate image that every piece of daily correspondence, whether an e-mail or a simple memo, must be perfect.

Some managers set no or conflicting writing standards, which results in confusion for their staffs and the need for time-consuming revisions that translate into higher production costs. Some provide no stylistic guidance or preference.

Sometimes it's more a question of style than correctness or quality of expression. After all, some people like meat; some prefer fish; still others eat only vegetables. Others like all three. Do not become overly self-critical. Do not beat yourself up or despair when your writing is once again returned marked up in red ink. Try to separate yourself from your writing; don't take it personally. Otherwise you may end up with an ulcer or high blood pressure or be forced to take a tranquilizer every time you submit your writing for your supervisor's approval.

One solution is to simply clarify your reviewer's goals and needs before you begin writing. Ask for advice and direction regarding important topics, which ideas to focus on, or even what not to say. Another solution is to review the criticism for either patterns of stylistic preferences (lists, short paragraphs, word choice) or concrete recurring problems in structure and usage (organization of ideas, spelling, grammar, punctuation) or in structure or content (tone, presentation of details). Keep copies of all correspondence and use them as models for similar assignments.

None of these techniques can guarantee total elimination of criticism nor ensure acceptance, but they will minimize the tendency for the former and enhance the likelihood of the latter.

9

Don't Trust the Spell-Checker: Proofreading Made Easier

*"I was working on the proof of one of my poems
all the morning, and took out a comma.
In the afternoon I put it back again."*
—Oscar Wilde

THE NEED TO PROOFREAD YOUR writing for mechanical correctness has to be one of most stressful, tedious, and unwelcome aspects of the writing process. Yet it's so essential to the quality of your work. The irony is that all the proofreading in the world cannot guarantee 100-percent correctness. Visit any bookstore, pick up and glance through any volume at random, and you are certain to find an error or two or more. The most prestigious newspapers and magazines will never be free of proofreading errors. Why not? Because as long as proofreading is done by people, there will always exist a margin for error. We are not perfect machines. In fact, even your well-intentioned spell-checker cannot help at times, especially when it comes to words such as *there* and *their* or *affect* and *effect*. Your spell-checker cannot be trusted to call attention to your inadvertently typing *form* when you intended to type *from* and that two plus two equals five.

Minimize Your Risk

Because no magic potion exists to guarantee total error-free writing, you can at least take steps to minimize the tendency all writers have to overlook embarrassing mistakes in correct usage. The first step is to distinguish the activity of proofreading from editing. Many writers regard them as one and the same when they are clearly as different as coffee and tea. One way to increase mechanical correctness is to avoid editing and proofreading at the same time. There is a tendency to become caught up with the content (what you want to say), as opposed to how it is physically presented, and so you miss errors. So either proofread or edit first. Don't try to do both. If you decide to proofread first, then preview the information to get a feel for the content. This approach will help you resist the temptation to become distracted by what you've attempted to express along the way.

Common Proofreading Errors

When you observe how many opportunities for error exist, it's no wonder that despite the most intensive, scrupulous proofreading, your final version will still be prone to a margin of mechanical error. Here is a list of the typical errors in need of correction when you proofread:

- Letter and space omission.
- Punctuation errors.
- Spelling errors.
- Grammar and usage errors.
- Transposed or substituted letters and words.
- Word and line omission.
- Lowercase instead of uppercase.
- Incorrect dates, telephone and fax numbers, or e-mail addresses.
- Reversed numbers in figures.

Visual Proofreading Techniques to Make Your Job Easier

Nothing can assure you that proofreading will be easy. However, the visual techniques that follow will help reduce the stress you may experience:

Previewing

First, skim or preview the document for a general impression of its content.

Line-by-Line Review

Carefully scan each line. For computer monitor readings, use the cursor or scroll key to help you focus on each word and line. To review printed versions, place a ruler, envelope, index card, or blank sheet of paper beneath each line to avoid being distracted by the rest of the text.

Reverse Line-by-Line Review

You may be skeptical attempting this technique, but it works because although you are reading backwards, you are not actually reading for meaning. As a result, your eye is more focused or trained upon observing the "physicality" of the words, their arrangement and spelling, and the presence and placement of punctuation marks.

Vertical Column Review

This technique is especially helpful when proofreading numerical data. Fold a hard copy of the page in half from top to bottom. Then proofread half the page beginning at the left margin and move your eyes downward. Then turn the page over and proofread from left to right and downwards from the point of folding. Do not worry about words overlapping the fold.

S-Pattern Review

Begin proofreading in the upper right-hand corner, and slowly move your eyes downward in a series of two or three S-patterns downwards and upwards over the entire page. It is most important to remember that none of these techniques will guarantee 100-percent mechanical correctness, but they will minimize the number of errors.

A Proofreading Checklist

In detective novels and movies, the hero must search for clues to lead him or her to the culprit. So too must the writer become a "proofreading detective," searching diligently and methodically for clues to the various mechanical errors (grammar, punctuation, spelling, usage, capitalization) that often occur in business writing. Here is a list of "clues"—that is, common errors that careful proofreading can help you detect and correct:

Incorrect Noun or Verb Endings

All engineer must writes weekly status reports.

Correct: All engineers must write weekly status reports.

Incorrect Subject/Verb Agreement

Each of the managers have to write a report.

Correct: Each of the managers has to write a report.

Incorrect Pronoun Reference

A person has a right to their opinion.

Correct: A person has a right to his or her opinion.

or

People have a right to their opinions.

Correct Use of Who, That, and Which

Remember that *who* refers to people and *that* and *which* can refer to people or objects. When editing sentences for punctuation, insert commas around *nonrestrictive* or nonessential clauses (groups of words that do not limit the meaning, often introduced by "who" or "which") but not around *restrictive* or essential ones (often introduced by "that").

Nonrestrictive

My cousin Carlo, *who is a lawyer,* won the lottery.

Because Carlo's occupation is not important or essential to the main idea within the sentence, the phrase "who is a lawyer" is set off by commas.

Restrictive

The car *that Jerry bought in California* is 10 years old.

Because the phrase "that Jerry bought in California" limits and is essential to the meaning of the sentence, this phrase is not set off by commas.

Split Infinitives or Verb Phrases

An infinitive consists of the word *to* plus the basic or root form of the verb, such as "to climb." Review your sentences for occasions when you have split the infinitive, such as this:

Split

Mel expected to soon join Linda in Boston.

Correct

Mel expected to join Linda soon in Boston.

Separated or Missing Words and Phrases

Confusing

While sitting on the sofa, the phone rang.

Clear

While I was sitting on the sofa, the phone rang.

Vague

Joe wrote a letter to his brother waiting in the train station for Chris to arrive.

Precise

Waiting at the train station for Chris to arrive, Joe wrote a letter to his brother.

Misleading

I walk only to work in the summer.

Correct

I walk to work only in the summer.

Substitutions and Omissions

Next Friday is an important holyday (holiday).

Jane sent me (an) important message this morning.

Errors in Numerical Accuracy

The total amount due is $1952 (19.52).

CAUTION: Always check carefully for totals, percentages, fractions, and placement of decimal points.

Errors in Preferred Spelling of Names

Please fax this invoice to Mrs. Iris White (Whyte).

Transpositions of Letters, Numbers, and Words

Last week Nick drove form (from) New York to Atlanta in one day.

Send this package to 3880 (3088) Stratford Green Lane.

Punctuation Error

As requested; (,) here is a copy of our new procedures.

Grammar and Usage Errors

Between you and I (me), this is a rare opportunity.

Each of the engineers have (has) contributed to the new project.

Capitalization and Number Errors

Dave has worked for IbM (IBM).

Order 105' (10 five-foot) boards.

Inconsistencies in Format, Line Spacing, and/or Typography (font, point size, italics, bold face)

We appreciate your contacting us about our service department.

10

E-mail: To Send or Not to Send?

*"Writing, when properly managed is but
a different name for conversation."*

—Laurence Sterne

WOULD YOU WANT TO RECEIVE this e-mail?

TO: ALL SUPERVISORS
FROM: JOEL CAIRO

HURRICANE RAOUL IS ABOUT 200 MILES SOUTH OF CHARLESTON, S.C. HE IS STILL A CATEGORY 5 HURRICANE WITH SUSTAINED WINDS OF 175 MPH...GUSTS TO 220.

HE IS MOVING NORTH BY NORTHWEST VERY SPEEDILY AND WILL ARRIVE HERE BY MIDNIGHT. THE HURRICANE CENTER EXPECTS RAOUL TO MOVE ACROSS SOUTH CAROLINA AND THEN UP THE EAST COAST THRU ATLANTIC CITY AND POINTS NORTH TO BOSTON BEFORE TRACKING WESTWARD HO. WE THINK THE TRACK WILL CONTINUE NORTH BUT WHO ARE WE TO QUESTION THE EXPERTS AT THE NATIONAL WEATHER BUREAU. AFTER ALL, THEY HIRED MY BROTHER-IN-LAW SO HOW GOOD CAN THEY REALLY BE? THIS IS INDEED AS STRONG A TROPICAL STORM AS WE CAN EVER HOPE TO SEE IN OUR PART OF THE COUNTRY. THEN AGAIN IT MIGHT PETER OUT AND ALL THIS FUSS WILL HAVE BEEN FOR NOTHING. BUT

RIGHT NOW WE KNOW THAT WINDS WILL STEADILY
INCREASE AND BE STRONGEST AROUND MIDNIGHT.
LOTS OF RAIN AND THUNDERSTORMS EXPECTED
ALONG WITH THIS STORM. THE STORM IS EXPECTED
TO MOVE OUT OF THE REGION BY TOMORROW AF-
TERNOON BUT IN THE MEANTIME COASTAL AREAS
WILL HAVE TO BE CAREFULLY MONITORED AND ALL
SAFETY PRECAUTIONS REGARDING PERSONNEL,
EQUIPMENT AND FACILITIES MUST BE TAKEN.

Wouldn't you rather receive this one?

TO: All Supervisors
FROM: J. Cairo

Hurricane Raoul is expected to arrive here by midnight. Thunderstorms and rain will accompany this storm
until it moves out of the area by late afternoon tomorrow.

Please take immediate appropriate precautions regarding personnel, vulnerable outdoor equipment, and facilities.

Subject Lines

During an average business day your reader most likely
receives numerous e-mail messages. The challenge is for you
to capture your reader's attention and then to maintain it so
your reader will respond to or act upon your message.

 Guidelines to Composing Power E-mail

- Understand the guidelines/principles of power e-mail.
- Create precise attention-getting subject lines.
- Be aware of first impressions: The importance of the
  opening sentence.
- Organize e-mail content for easier reading.
- Edit e-mail for clarity and precision.
- Use appropriate professional tone.
- Prefer gender-free language.

An effective subject line:

- Attracts your reader's attention.
- Provides an accurate, precise description of your subject.

Here are some examples of weak and imprecise subject lines:

- Loading Problems
- Customer Service
- Software Demo Class

Here are some examples of precise subject lines:

- Container Loading Problems for Vessel "Northern Star" (June 10)
- Revised Customer Service Procedures
- New Accounting Software Demo Class Schedule

First Impressions

The ancient Greek playwright Euripides wrote: "A bad beginning makes a bad ending."

More than 2,000 years later this rule aptly applies to e-mail. A strong opening sentence is especially important in e-mail messages to motivate your busy readers to follow the document through to its conclusion. The lead sentence expresses your main idea, focus of discussion, or immediate needs as briefly, concisely and accurately as possible. Remember: If you lose your readers' attention in the beginning you've lost them entirely. They may never return to understand the essence of your otherwise important message.

Here are some examples of weak and strong opening sentences and paragraphs:

Weak Opening

This is in response to the message I received from you concerning the best time for us to meet in your office to discuss ways to improve safety procedures at our plant.

According to my and Evan Douglas's schedule the best time to meet would be this Friday at 2. Let me know if this is convenient for you.

Strong Opening

Evan Douglas and I can meet with you at 2 p.m. on Friday, April 5, to discuss plant safety procedures. Please let me know if this date and time are convenient for you.

Weak Opening

The purpose of this e-mail is to inform you that the Maintenance Department will begin work on the following list of various outdoor repairs on June 28 but you need to know that all this depends on the weather because as you know it has been a wet month. So it is important to bear in mind that the following list of repairs may not be completed as scheduled for July 10.

Strong Opening

The Maintenance Department will begin work on the outdoor repairs listed below on June 28.

If good weather prevails, we expect to complete the work by July 10.

Organizing Messages

In most e-mail messages, always provide the most important information first. Visualize the details of your message as sections of an inverted pyramid, with the base representing the opening sentence and the tip the least essential or minor details. For busy executives, structure the writing to begin with a summary or the conclusions/recommendations and provide the details to be read optional. In presenting your message, organize information according to one of the following patterns:

- Cause/Effect.
- Problem/Solution.

- Comparison/Contrast.
- Chronology/Sequence of Events.

Another helpful method to organize ideas is to ask your-self and answer these questions to increase the odds you will provide an adequate number of specific, supporting details essential to your reader fully comprehending your message:

- Who?
- What?
- When?
- Where?
- Why?
- How?

Conversational Professional Language Style

Aside from speed of transmission, one great benefit of e-mail is its encouragement of conversational language. Yet the way we speak and write holds numerous differ-ences. In speech, we pause, vary our tone, convey mean-ing through facial expressions and body language, have the opportunity to quickly address our listener's apparent confusion or misunderstanding, and use vague or broad terms rather than specific precise ones. So the challenge, then, in writing e-mail, is to strike a balance between lan-guage style that seems conversational but in fact is written and language that is precise and professional. It is impor-tant to remember that the same truths that apply to tradi-tional memos, letters, and reports apply to e-mail: Clarity and precision are indispensable to the successful recep-tion of your message. Moreover, when writing e-mail, an-other important consideration is whether the tone of your conversational style is appropriate to your purpose and con-tent and within the bounds of standard writing etiquette. Here are some principles to bear in mind:

1. Aside from the formal documents sent via e-mail (contracts, proposals, business plans) use contractions selectively. After all, we use them in speech.

   INSTEAD OF:

   I shall call you if the package does not arrive by noon on Friday.

   WRITE:

   I'll call you if the package doesn't arrive by noon on Friday.

2. Use personal pronouns such as *I, we,* and *you* to convey directness, vigorous tone, and sense of immediacy. Avoid using "one" (too impersonal and often pontifical).

   INSTEAD OF:

   One should be able to complete the test in one hour.

   WRITE:

   You should be able to complete the test in one hour.

3. Although you should avoid ending sentences with prepositions, it's okay to do so to avoid excessively formal constructions in e-mail and casual correspondence.

   INSTEAD OF:

   With whom are you attending the meeting?

   WRITE:

   Who are you attending the meeting with?

Prefer Words That Project a Conversational Tone

The following list of words compares formal and sometimes awkward constructions and word choices with those that suggest greater informality and ease of tone:

Formal	Informal
are found to be in agreement	agree
as per request	as requested
attached please find	attached is/are
begin implementation	start using
effectuate improvement	improve
is indicative of	indicates, reveals
it would be appreciated	please, I would appreciate
kindly furnish	please send/submit
make mention of	mention
obtain an increase in	increase
optimum	most, best
patronage	business
perform an evaluation	evaluate
pursuant to	in regards to
reference is made	in reference to
remuneration	payment
should this necessitate	if this needs
show an illustration of	illustrate, show
utilize	use

Ensuring Clarity and Precision

E-mail is not radically different from traditional written business correspondence. Rather, e-mail employs an electronic medium to convey the message instantly. For the busy reader, short sentences are easier to write and read. Long sentences take more time and have a greater tendency to bury or delay main messages and details. Readers are more likely to "trash" e-mail that never gets to the point or is characterized by excessive mechanical errors and confusing meaning. Clarity, precision, and appropriate tone are essential to ensuring that your e-mail is well-received and understood by all readers. Before sending any e-mail message, whether internal or external, always take the time to edit for content and structure.

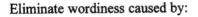
Eliminate wordiness caused by:

Fancy/unfamiliar words

We need to promulgate (announce) the new safety procedures to all personnel.

 General Guidelines for Successful E-Mail

1. Consider your reader's needs and the amount of background necessary to understand your message. If you're responding to an earlier message, paraphrase as concisely as possible the key ideas.

2. Keep sentences short (25 words max) but complete (one idea per sentence). Do not write fragment sentences.

3. Provide a subject line for each message.

4. Limit each message to one subject.

5. Organize your ideas in short paragraphs (three to five sentences) separated by one blank space.

6. Maintain a professional, businesslike tone. Read the message from the reader's point of view at least once to ensure an appropriate tone of voice and to minimize opportunities for misunderstanding.

7. Do not use all capital or lowercase letters in your sentences. Follow standard English guidelines to capitalization you would use in traditional business correspondence.

8. Do not send messages composed in anger or in direct response to insulting messages.

9. Do not use humor the reader could interpret as inappropriate to the content or occasion.

10. Prefer simple concrete words when writing to someone for whom English is a second language. These readers tend to translate word for word and there is a greater chance for misunderstanding if you use acronyms, abbreviations, cliches, slang, jargon, or regional expressions limited to American English. (For example, 1/5/03 is May 1, 2003 to Europeans.)

11. Edit and proofread for correct spelling, grammar, punctuation, capitalization, and usage.

Excessively Long Phrases and Expressions

Due to the fact (Because) your purchase order was misplaced, attached herewith please find (attached is) a coupon for a 10 percent discount towards your next order.

Smothered Verbs

Our department will effectuate improvement (improve) of sanitary conditions in the cafeteria.

Passive Voice

By now, the memo by Hadley Peters regarding hiring additional personnel has been received by all intended recipients.

Unnecessary Prepositional Phrases

The Accounting Department is known for the preparation of (for preparing) easy-to-read instructions.

Tone

It is important to remember that, although e-mail reflects a casual and informal style, it must still maintain a professional image and tone. The immediacy of e-mail communication can tempt you to inappropriate displays of emotion and anger and the use of obscene (even in jest) or abusive language. However familiar you may be with your reader, corporate e-mail must reflect a formal cordiality, dignity, and seriousness of purpose. Do not use e-mail as a shield to hide behind personal hostility or to convey negative news you feel uncomfortable conveying in person.

Also, if you receive an upsetting or insulting message, do not respond immediately. No matter how justified your response may be, you will appear the aggressor who is out of control. You can ensure that you convey the appropriate tone by:

1.   *Considering* your relationship with the reader. Is it familiar? Positive? Friendly? Tense? Formal? Business?

2.   *Identifying* the reader's likely point of view, needs, expectations, concerns, possible biases, attitudes, and interests.

3.   *Determining* the primary purpose of your e-mail. Does your message have more than one purpose? If so, either clearly distinguish each purpose in your opening or write separate e-mail messages to avoid confusion or ambiguity.

4.   *Understanding* how much detail the reader will need (time, dates, examples, addresses, names) to avoid information-overload.

5.   *Asking* if and how much the reader may care about the content of your e-mail. Consider the extent of the beneficial appeal of the e-mail to the reader's interest, needs, decision-making, and understanding of process, instructions, and incident.

6.   *Placing* yourself in the reader's position. Would you want to receive and have to read your own e-mail?

Gender-Free Language

Language always reflects changing times, and nowhere is change more apparent than in the need to prefer gender-free references. Women are increasingly assuming senior managerial and executive positions in the corporate and political world. As a result, e-mail should be free of words and phrases that by modern standards appear archaic and at worst insulting and insensitive. Here are some ways to keep the language in your e-mail gender-free:

Eliminate the Masculine Pronoun

A manager needs to express (his) ideas with clarity and precision.

Use a Noun

We always provide (a man) the customer with personal attention.

Use Plural Nouns and Pronouns

Editors must have a sound knowledge of English usage.

Use "He/She" or "His or Her" Combined Pronouns

A person has a right to his or her opinion.

Use Passive Voice

How often must a scientist perform this experiment to obtain the correct result?

Editing and Proofreading

If you are unable to resist the temptation to hit the "send" button upon completing your first draft and neglect to edit or proofread, chances are your professional image will suffer greatly. Your reader will not understand that you are too important or busy to carefully review your message for content and mechanical correctness. The impression will be of someone too lazy or careless to produce a polished message. E-mail sent "before its time" will always reflect negatively on both your and the company's professional image. So no matter how busy or seemingly informal the message, take a few minutes to ask the following editorial questions:

1. Why am I writing this message? What do I hope or need to accomplish?
2. How much does the reader already know or need to know about my topic?
3. Is technical knowledge or an understanding of industry jargon necessary?
4. Does the reader have a biased, negative, or distrustful opinion of the subject matter?

5. Might others read the message?
6. Is my purpose clearly expressed in the subject line?
7. Have I clearly identified my reason for writing to the reader?
8. Did I emphasize the important points?
9. Do the ideas flow logically?
10. Did I use fancy, unfamiliar words?
11. Are my sentences and paragraphs too long?
12. Is my tone informal but professional?
13. Did I write too many passive voice sentences?
14. Did I check for redundant words?
15. Did I use headings and lists to help organize my thoughts?
16. Are there mistakes in spelling, capitalization, grammar, punctuation, and usage?
17. Would I want to receive this message as written?

E-Mail Shorthand List

Here is a list of e-mail abbreviations and acronyms you may encounter:

Acronym	Meaning
2U2	To You Too
AAMOF	As a Matter of Fact
AFAIK	As Far as I Know
AFAIC	As Far as I'm Concerned
AFAICT	As Far as I Can Tell
ASAP	As Soon as Possible
BBL	Be Back Later
BITMT	But in the Meantime
BRB	Be Right Back
BTW	By the Way
CU	See You
CUL8R	See You Later
CWOT	Complete Waste of Time

Acronym	Meaning
CYA	See You
EOD	End of Discussion
EZ	Easy
FAQ	Frequently Asked Question
FBOW	For Better or Worse
FOCL	Falling Off Chair Laughing
FWIW	For What It's Worth
FYA	For Your Amusement
FYI	For Your Information
GBTW	Get Back to Work
GFC	Going for Coffee
GFETE	Grinning From Ear to Ear
GMTA	Great Minds Think Alike
GTG	Got to Go
GTGTTBR	Got to Go to the Bathroom
GTRM	Going to Read Mail
HAND	Have a Nice Day
HTH	Hope This Helps
IAC	In any Case
IAE	In any Event
IC	I See
IDGI	I Don't Get It
IMCO	In My Considered Opinion
IMHO	In My Humble Opinion
IMO	In My Opinion
IOW	In Other Words
IRL	In Real Life
IYKWIM	If You Know What I Mean
JIC	Just in Case
J/K	Just Kidding
KISS	Keep It Simple Stupid
L8TR	Later
LOL	Laughing Out Loud
LTNS	Long Time No See
MTCW	My Two Cents Worth
NRN	No Reply Necessary

Acronym	Meaning
ONNA	Oh No, Not Again
OTOH	On the Other Hand
OTTOMH	Off The Top of My Head
OIC	Oh I See
PLS	Please
PU	That Stinks
ROFL	Rolling on Floor Laughing
ROTFL	Rolling on the Floor Laughing
ROTF	Rolling on the Floor
RSN	Real Soon Now
RTD	Read the Directions
RUOK	Are You Okay?
SNAFU	Situation Normal; All Fouled Up
SOL	Smiling Out Loud
TANSTAAFL	There Ain't No Such Thing as a Free Lunch
TAFN	That's All For Now
THX	Thanks
TIA	Thanks in Advance
TLK2UL8R	Talk to You Later
TMK	To My Knowledge
TPTB	The Powers That Be
TTBOMK	To the Best of My Knowledge
TTFN	Ta-Ta For Now
TWIMC	To Whom It May Concern
WB	Welcome Back
WRT	With Regard To
WU?	What's Up?
YGIAGAM	Your Guess Is as Good as Mine
YGWYPF	You Get What You Pay For
ZZZ	Sleeping

11

Memo, Letter, and Report Guidelines

"This is what I'd like to put in my letter: 'Beautiful Marquise, your beautiful eyes make me die of love,' but I'd like to put it in an elegant way."

—Moliere

Memos

MEMOS CONVEY INFORMATION WITHIN AN organization. The purpose of the message can be to inform, instruct, advise, announce, remind, respond to questions or concerns, offer answers to inquiries and solutions to problems, express appreciation or, report on meetings or status of ongoing projects. Memos can be informal or formal in wording and tone and distributed to all personnel within a company or to a select group. Because memos often address specific topics, they include subject lines. Nowadays in many companies, information previously communicated through paper memos is conveyed through e-mail. When planning a memo, whether intended to be sent via paper or electronically, it is helpful to ask the following:

- What is the main idea of my message?
- Who will be receiving the memo?
- How much background should I provide?

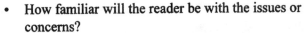

- How familiar will the reader be with the issues or concerns?
- Is the content intended for technical and non-technical personnel?
- Will any immediate or future action be required of the reader?

When writing the memo:

- State your message in the first sentence or paragraph.
- Provide necessary background or frame of reference.
- List specific dates, times, locations, details, figures, data, suggestions, guidelines, and so forth in order of importance.
- If necessary close with urge to act (call, meet, advise, submit information).

Example: Announcement Memo

DATE: February 20, 20—
TO: Gerry Connelly
FROM: Anthony Ramos
SUBJECT: Safety Awareness Workshop

In order to meet the requirements of our new Safety and Security Procedures, a series of half-day workshops designed to enhance personal safety awareness of all employees will be offered on March 15, April 5, and June 10 at our headquarters training center, Room 200. The workshops will be presented by Lenny Clark, Director of Safety. All workshops will begin promptly at 9 a.m. and end at 12 p.m. Breakfast and lunch will be provided.

Please notify Kathy Wolfe at ext. 3088 of the date you will attend this workshop.

Example: Memo Suffering From Information-Overload

If you've ever tried stacking cartons you may have experienced what happens when too many are placed on top of the rest. The same collapse results when the reader is overloaded with information. Here is an example:

TO: All personnel
FROM: Enrique Moderna
SUBJECT: Casual Dress Codes

We are frequently being asked what our official policy is regarding proper business casual dress attire. Because styles and tastes change with each season year in and year out, and everything that was once old seems to truly become new again, it is no wonder so many of you are uncertain of what exactly constitutes proper business casual attire. I believe that we have finally settled upon some guidelines, informal and certainly not carved in granite or marble or even cardboard for that matter, that will prove helpful to those of you so perplexed about how to dress for work.

Because it would be highly impractical to list a definitive list of what is acceptable and what is not, it appears permissible to state that the clothing employees select to wear during business hours depends entirely upon the type of daily activity and job function. Employees are expected to exercise good taste, judgment, and plain common sense when trying to decide what to wear. Everyone should be groomed in a manner befitting the professional image he or she wishes to project and yet not be extreme in one way or the other. T-shirts, blue jeans, sandals, sneakers, shorts, and tank tops are not acceptable at any time. For specifics, consult your department head.

🖉🖉🖉

Here's a revised version:

TO: All personnel
FROM: Enrique Moderna
SUBJECT: Casual Dress Codes

I realize that daily casual business attire is largely a matter of personal style and taste. At the same time, employees are expected to exercise good judgment in deciding what to wear to work. Please remember that T-shirts, blue jeans, sandals, sneakers, shorts, tank tops, and exercise clothing are not acceptable at any time. Because clothes often make the man or woman, we expect everyone to arrive to work wearing clothing that allows for comfort yet reflects a professional image.

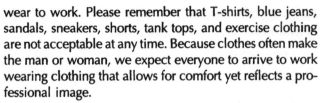

Following are examples of some common types of daily memos:

Informative Memo

TO: All Financial Analysts
FROM: Fran Cesco
DATE: 2/28
SUBJECT: Environmental Laws and Regulations

Our company is subject to numerous federal, state, and local environmental laws and regulations governing air emissions, waste water discharge, solid and hazardous waste treatment, and storage, disposal, and remediation of releases of hazardous materials.

In common with much of the mining industry, our facilities are located on sites used for heavy industrial purposes for decades. Because subsequent remediation is therefore likely, environmental laws may become more strictly enforced in the future, and we can expect costs of compliance to increase.

Request/Recommendation Memo

TO: S. Dalton
FROM: M. J. Lowell
DATE: 1/12
SUBJECT: Test Reports

In recent months, submission of test reports for new products has been continually well beyond the required deadline. These late submissions have resulted in extensive delays in the approval process required for each submission.

Please advise all research personnel that late submissions of their test reports is no longer acceptable.

Effective immediately, all test reports must be submitted to my office no later than the 15th of each month.

Procedure Memo

TO: Margo Lindsay
FROM: Donna Bayley
DATE: 8/19
SUBJECT: Training Requests

Please comply with the following procedures for requesting training for your staff:

1. Submit a brief statement to my office describing both the need and relevance of the specific training to the prospective participant's job responsibilities.
2. Describe the benefits of the training of individual needs, practical application to daily job responsibilities, professional growth, job performance, and productivity.
3. If more than three individuals request attending the same training program, schedule the additional personnel for the earliest next training session.

Please call Gerri Lane (ext. 1225) for further information regarding these procedures.

Memo Report Discussing a Problem

TO: All personnel
FROM: M. Simone
DATE: 3/15
SUBJECT: Equipment Damage Problem

Recently, I received the Equipment Damage Claim Report distributed by Carmine D'Angelo for the first quarter. The rising costs of equipment damage, which have increased 56 percent compared with last year, are most disturbing. Such a substantial increase should serve as a warning that an increase in incidents could also result in an increase in personal injuries. As a result, we need to begin intensifying all employees' awareness of the seriousness of this issue.

As it has been my experience when attending safety meetings to observe that there is not enough discussion about equipment damage, it is imperative that this issue be addressed in future meetings. It is only when reducing equipment damage becomes a high priority concern that we will begin to make progress towards reducing lost time cases and the potential for personal injury.

Memo or E-Mail of Welcome

TO: J. Kane
FROM: C. Gandy
DATE: 10/31
SUBJECT: Welcome

Welcome to El Moldo Cat Foods. We are very happy to welcome you as a new member of our outstanding Research and Development Department. Please be assured that at El Moldo we will value your distinguished expertise and reward your contributions to enhancing the quality of our product.

We will provide you with every opportunity to fully realize your professional potential and goals.

If I can be of assistance to you at any time, please call me at ext. 819.

Recording/Reporting Meeting Minutes

Have you ever uttered these or similar words to yourself: "Meetings, meetings, meetings. Nothing but meetings all day. How do they expect me to get anything done if I have to go to all these meetings?" I like to think of meetings as the commercials of everyday business life. Many are important and informative; others may appear unnecessary to all but the person who called the meeting. I cannot imagine anyone driving home from work who excitedly listens to a tape recording of a meeting. Can you?

If you are assigned the task of recording and reporting the minutes of a meeting, you almost have to transform yourself into a human tape recorder. Accuracy and objectivity are essential elements of your recorded comments, suggestions, agreements, conclusions, recommendations, planned actions, resolutions, and any other topic participants address. The details you record may often contain information that could have far-reaching implications, legal or otherwise. Your ability to record meeting minutes requires attention to detail and polished listening skills. You have to stay awake and alert, recording details and selectively editing at the same time.

There are a number of approaches to recording meeting minutes you will find helpful. The first is the ability to achieve distance and objectivity amidst your involvement. You must be able to participate in the activities of the moment and yet stay above the fray, so to speak. One technique is to position yourself in a corner of the room a short distance from the conference table. Do not face the group. The trick is to simultaneously be involved yet remain uninvolved in the discussions of various issues.

Your initial notes can take any form but must include the meeting's date, time, and agenda. The actual minutes can be recorded as a numbered list of issues/topics, or you can devise headings to reflect each item on the agenda. You can place quotation marks around record key comments or paraphrase them. You can underscore statements of fact or opinion, resolutions, recommendations, and future actions as you record them. Use headings to add a sense of order and structure to what initially will seem a chaotic mass of comments. Some writers prefer to record the information under the headings of "Minute 1, Minute 2," and so forth. If you use this format, also include headings. The sequence of issues can be presented according to the speaker's name.

Afterwards, assembling the notes into a well-organized document requires the same techniques of any other type of writing. What was the purpose of the meeting? Who attended? What were the major issues discussed? Were any resolutions determined? Were any actions suggested? Were there agreements or not regarding this or that issue? Was a follow-up meeting scheduled?

In your final version, before including any quoted comments, it is wise to ask those you are quoting to verify their comments. You don't want to find yourself in the awkward position of having someone accuse you of quoting him or her out of context. Also, whether the meeting is 15 minutes or an hour long your readers will appreciate your providing a summary of key points of discussion.

Memo Outlining Meeting Minutes

TO: Michael Martine

FROM: John Rocco

DATE: 5/27

SUBJECT: Meeting to Discuss the Status of Customer Service Center

On May 25, J. Rocco, E. Mars, and E. Cook met with representatives of Southern Builders to discuss the architectural design changes for the new Customer Service Center in Santa Rosa.

Pamela Carey, architect, and Gianna Lucia, Senior V-P, presented alternative views regarding lobby security, visitor parking, and landscaping. We found their suggestions acceptable and have advised them to submit formal design changes for our review by June 30.

Another meeting (June) is to be scheduled with representatives of Central Builders upon receipt of revised drawings. Initial construction of the Center is expected to begin four weeks following final approval of the design plans.

Letters

Letters are similar to memos and internal e-mail in their goals, which range from conveying information, instructions, policies, and decisions to requests for action. Letters are distinguished from internal e-mail messages and memos in their being sent to someone outside your organization whom you may or may not know. And there's the rub, to paraphrase Hamlet.

Letters are personal calling cards to your readers. Your initial correspondence with your reader offers a written first impression of you and your company. Depending upon how well it is written and your personal style, your reader either perceives someone who is reasonably intelligent, personable, competent, trustworthy, and skillful in written communication or gathers an instant negative impression. Letters allow you to talk with your reader and, just as we respond either positively or negatively to the tone of someone's telephone voice, so too will your reader react to your letter. Letters also reflect the company image.

Some years ago, I received a request from a large pharmaceutical company to teach editing and proofreading workshops. The training director explained how the president of the company had by chance come upon a letter written by a manager to a customer. There was one grammatical error, but one too many for him. The company president insisted the letter be rewritten but expressed gratitude for seeing the letter before it was mailed. His position was that the reader is unforgiving and so the company, not the writer, would be held up to ridicule. Perhaps he overreacted. Perhaps not, because what he said is still true. Your reader will judge both you and your organization based on the quality or lack of it in your letters.

Letter Style

Traditionally, letters for decades were written in what would seem to us today to be an overly formal manner. Here is an example of such letters:

May 27, 20—

Gentlemen:

Enclosed herewith please find payment for invoice in the amount of $45.00 submitted in response to letter of yours of the 28th April. We trust to be favored with your continued services and therefore remain, gentlemen, yours faithfully and with cordiality.

Sincerely,

Nowadays few readers would have the patience to read such verbose though ornately elegant sentences. In our time of cell phones and instantaneous e-mail, most readers have little time for such cordialities. They prefer the writer to get to the point.

May 27, 20—

Dear Ms. Smith:

Enclosed is payment of $45.00 for your invoice of April 28 for the repair service you provided. We look forward to continued business with your company.

Sincerely,

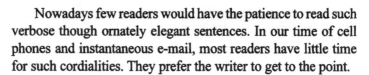

Here are suggested guidelines to apply when writing letters:

State your most important idea in the opening sentence or paragraph

February 5, 20—

Dear Ms. Thomas:

The results of the survey we conducted on January 20 reveal that a majority of your employees would enroll in training workshops presented onsite.

If responding to a letter, refer to its date or other identifying information

June 15, 20—

Dear Mr. Hansen:

In reply to your letter of March 4, please accept my apologies for the unsatisfactory service you experienced at our Cape Cod restaurant.

Offer minimal background or details to provide a frame of reference for your reader

July 10, 20—

Dear Mr. Marco:

I submitted your resume to Grace Marti, Director of Information Technology, and she has expressed an interest in meeting with you next week to discuss your background.

Emphasize key ideas and details, underline important words

November 4, 20—

Dear Mrs. Brown:

In response to your inquiry of October 30, the general principle involved in the typography of datelines, addresses, and signatures is that they should be set to stand out clearly from the body of the letter. This is accomplished by using CAPS and *italics*.

Present information in order of importance

August 19, 20—

Dear Mr. Marcial:

I have recently learned that only a small percentage of your employees have enrolled in a retirement plan offered by our investment firm.

It appears that many are skeptical about investing in stocks and bonds because of the unfortunate experiences of one of your managers who lost a substantial amount of money last year, which resulted from his investing in highly speculative stocks.

I would be willing to have one of our representatives offer a brief talk about the various forms of investments that would offer both safety and potential growth.

If you are interested in scheduling this presentation, please call me toll free at 1-800-123-4567.

Sincerely,

Use headings, numbered or bulleted lists, and/or single sentences to highlight major points

May 10, 20—

Dear Ms. Marquettte:

In response to your inquiry regarding plant names and forms, I have compiled the following list of guidelines for indicating plant names.

1. In general, derivatives of proper names with acquired independent meaning are not capitalized.
2. If the capital letter is retained, either the hyphenated or the two-word form is used, depending on predominant

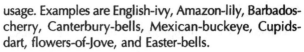
usage. Examples are English-ivy, Amazon-lily, Barbados-cherry, Canterbury-bells, Mexican-buckeye, Cupids-dart, flowers-of-Jove, and Easter-bells.

3. Such names as Charlie, Jack, and Susan lose their capital letters. Examples are jack-in-the-pulpit, black-eyed-susan, and creeping-charlie.

4. The apostrophe is omitted in names with a possessive element. Examples are Grays lily, Jacobs-rod, ladies-tresses, Queen-Annes-lace, and Turks-cap.

5. Preferred usage applies to those plants indicated by adjective forms rather than by plant names. These include may-apple, blackbud, beebalm, bigmoon, dawnrose, halfmoon.Usually though not without exception, plant names ending in bane, bark, bean, berry, bine, brush, cup, fern, flower, grass, leaf, lily, nut, pea, plant, pod, root, seed, thorn, tree, vine, weed, wood and wort are printed as solid words. Examples are bluestem, chainfern, blackberry.

6. Usually though not without exception, plant names ending in bane, bark, bean, berry, bine, brush, cup, fern, flower, grass, leaf, lily, nut, pea, plant, pod, root, seed, thorn, tree, vine, weed, wood and wort are printed as solid words. Examples are bluestem, chainfern, blackberry.

Note: If the preceding word is a proper name which retains its capitalized form, the name is hyphenated, as in Australian-pea.

I hope you will find this information helpful and appreciate your writing us.

Sincerely,

Maintain a cordial, professional tone

Perhaps the billing error was the result of an oversight.

Prefer active voice sentences

I will send the report to you tomorrow.

Avoid cliches

You're barking up the wrong tree.

In your closing, state clearly any requests for action from your reader

Please submit your request no later than August 10.

Avoid Beginning a Letter With:

1. Unnecessary or inappropriate general statements.

> How's the weather in Phoenix?

2. Obvious references or statements.

- I am writing this letter to....
- This letter is in reference to...

3. Archaic and legal-sounding words and phrases.

- Attached hereto...
- Reference is made...
- Pursuant to...
- I acknowledge receipt of your letter.

Reports

The idea of writing a report can cause alarm for any writer. When you are assigned the task of writing a report, your first thought may likely be, "This is going to take time or involve a lot of work." Writing a report is not something you dash off in a minute or two, such as an e-mail or fax. The very official nature of most reports can be daunting in terms of our reader's expectations and the need to convey information objectively and convincingly. Reports take time, whether in gathering the facts and details or in the actual writing. They can be less stressful if you use the following approach:

Step 1: Determine the Purpose

The first step is to determine the goal or purpose of writing the report. Will it be used for information, decision-making, problem-solving, understanding reasons for an existing problem instruction, measure progress, auditing, or explaining a process or procedure? Knowing what you do not have to address in the report is as helpful as deciding what is essential.

Suggested Opening Lines

- Here is the information you requested in your recent letter.
- Enclosed is a copy of our annual report.
- We have carefully investigated the incident you reported and have found....
- I would like to offer my services to your organization.
- Thank you for applying for the position of senior health care specialist.
- I would appreciate your help in providing/obtaining the following information.
- I can understand how frustrated you felt when you realized the sweater you received was the wrong size.
- We are pleased to welcome you as a preferred banking customer.
- Thank you for letting us know about the difficulty you encountered attempting to assemble our E-Z bookcase.
- Please allow me to express my regrets at the unfortunate rudeness you experienced at our store.
- I understand you are seeking someone experienced with the XYZ system.
- Please accept my apologies for responding late.
- We are concerned that your monthly payment is 90 days past due.
- This is to confirm your appointment at 10 a.m. on Friday, July 5, with our account representative.
- Congratulations on your promotion to Director of Marketing.
- I would be glad to meet with you on Thursday, August 18 at 4 p.m.
- I agree you should have received your refund several weeks ago.
- We've noticed you haven't used your Flying Club mileage privileges.
- Mr. George Thomas has asked me to reply to your letter of November 12 concerning customer-service procedures.

Suggested Opening Lines *(cont.)*

- I am extremely disappointed with your not providing the materials we needed to complete construction of our research and development center.
- Have you received the two catalogues I sent you last Monday?
- I'm writing to invite you to join our tennis club.
- Here is a list of our training goals.
- I am very sorry to learn of your recent accident.
- Please follow these instructions carefully.
- Here are the instructions for operating the new lawn mower.
- Diana Baker has suggested I contact you for information about your firm's legal services.
- Please cancel my order.
- We have received your payment of $190.
- This report summarizes our test results.
- I have forwarded your letter to our accounts payable department.
- Thank you for taking the time to write us about our products.
- Many thanks for the helpful suggestions you offered. I would appreciate your help in solving a problem with the new software.
- I have learned that several employees are taking three-hour lunches.
- Did you ever receive the faxes I sent last week?
- According to our benefits guidelines, you will be fully reimbursed for the tests.
- If there's any other way I can help you, please call me immediately.

Step 2: Identify Your Reader

In everything we write we need to consider the reader. This is especially true when preparing a report because of the

Suggested Closing Lines

- If we can be of further service, please let us know.
- I very much enjoyed meeting with you.
- Thank you for your patience and understanding.
- I look forward to hearing from you.
- We will work with you to resolve this urgent matter.
- Thank you for taking the time to meet with me.
- Please call or write to make payment arrangements.
- Many thanks for the gracious welcome.
- Please send a copy of the corrected invoice to the address listed below.
- Your payment of $145 will bring your account current.
- Please sign and return the enclosed contract.
- I am hoping you will feel better with each day.
- Here's how you can help us raise funds.
- It was thoughtful of you to include us in your celebration.
- You should receive your new computer within five business days.Thank you for your order.
- We appreciate your continued business.
- Please read this prospectus carefully before investing in our fund.
- I would appreciate hearing from you no later than Friday.
- Please express my best wishes to Mary Jane.
- If you have any questions about the project, please call me.

considerable amount of potentially complex information a report may include. Here are some questions to ask:

- What is the reader's interest in the report?
- Will the report be submitted to readers with different needs and levels of understanding?
- How knowledgeable is the reader about the subject of the report?

- Does the reader share your professional or technical expertise?
- How much background information will be necessary?
- Is the reader in or outside your organization?
- Will the reader need to understand particular theories or technical data included in the report?
- Will the reader have the time, interest, or ability to review any technical data?
- Do you need to explain technical terms and methods?
- Should you provide illustrations to support the text?
- Should you provide explanatory text for the illustrations?
- Will your reader find a summary helpful?
- Can extensive supporting data be placed an appendix rather than in the body of your report?

Step 3: Organize the Information

The information presented in a report can be organized according to one of the following patterns or formats:

- Sequence or Time Order.
- Problem/Solution.
- Cause/Effect.
- Function.
- Procedure.
- Progress.
- Importance.

Step 4: Decide Which Elements to Include

Reports can be informal or formal depending on your purpose, the nature of the information, and your relationship with the reader. Informal reports may concern routine assignments such as field trips or tests and can consist of one to two pages. The information can be general or detailed, depending on your knowledge of the reader's needs and expectations and whether the report is intended for those inside or outside an organization.

If you are familiar with your reader, you may prefer to use a conversational presentation style and not feel the need to explain technical terms or acronyms your reader already understands. The informal report consists of a title, summary, introduction and brief background, supporting details, and a conclusion or recommendation. Formal reports often treat a subject extensively and are prepared for a select audience, such as the company president, board of directors, shareholders, executive committee, investigative body, or client. As a result, formal reports will consist of information that needs to be presented in a more structured format. Because these reports may not be routine assignments and there is less chance you will be familiar with your readers, the tone is more impersonal and there is greater need for explaining terms and data and perhaps for including illustrations to support or explain your findings. You can arrange the information according to the following pattern:

- Provide a *letter of transmittal* or cover letter to explain the purpose of the report, the subject, benefits of the findings or data reported, limitations or obstacles encountered, and importance or value to the reader.
- Include a *title page* that announces your report's subject or focus in specific words.

  Instead of:

  Training Procedures

  Write:

  New Training Procedures for Customer Service Personnel

- Provide a *table of contents*.
- Begin with a *summary* of key points in layman's terms. Do not use *technical* jargon, acronyms, abbreviations, scientific formulas, or mathematical calculations or principles.
- Present an *introduction* that outlines the subject, purpose, and scope of the report.
- State *background* details as briefly as possible. Place highly detailed background information that is not required by all readers in an appendix.

- Present a *discussion* of your key ideas and findings along with supporting details in a series of paragraphs listed in order of importance.
- List *conclusions, recommendations, solutions,* or an *urge to act* in your closing statement.
- Provide *appendices* consisting of a *glossary, bibliography, list of symbols,* and any additional information that will be helpful to your readers.

Evaluative Report Example

TERM LOAN FACILITATION: XYZ International

Executive Summary

Based in Chicago, XYZ International is the leading producer of cement in the Midwest. XYZ International is engaged primarily in the production, distribution, marketing, and sales of cement and ready-mix concrete. XYZ is seeking to expand its market share of business in Canada and Mexico, and is seeking to acquire two major cement producers. As such, Lazzo and Partners has been asked to arrange a $10 million financing Term Loan.

Background

The cement producing industry has experienced considerable growth in the last decade, largely due to new home and commercial office construction, extensive bridge and highway repairs, and numerous other public works programs. In the last two years, cement consumption increased 59 percent throughout the United States as a result of increasing new housing starts and low interest rates.

In the last 10 years, XYZ has expanded into markets through geographic diversification. For the year ended, XYZ derived approximately 49 percent from midwestern sales, 21 percent from southwest sales, 16 percent from northwestern sales and 14 percent from southeastern sales.

Investment Merits and Risks

As a result of the positive trends that have been occurring in the cement production industry, XYZ appears to be in an excellent position to grow and expand its share of the market. The company has been generating strong cash flow and has been showing significant operating profitability during the last five years. In addition, the company has built up sufficient cash to be prepared to take advantage of opportunities to purchase smaller companies at reasonable prices.

Moreover, XYZ has restructured any outstanding debt to reduce interest expense (from 8.5 percent to 5.25 percent) and improve its financial strength. The company has an experienced management team capable of adapting to changing market trends. Demand for cement consumption is expected to continue in all market areas.

At the same time, although the immediate outlook for cement consumption appears favorable, continued strong marketplace demand is uncertain. Interest rates may rise, housing starts may reach surplus levels, funds for public works programs may be decreased. Competition from foreign cement producers, such as Domingo, S.A., which has strong sales in southwestern states that include Texas, New Mexico, Nevada, and Arizona, is likely to continue and may lead to declining sales and prices. It also remains to be seen how the market for cement consumption performs according to economic fluctuations.

Recommendations

Management believes that given the strong indicators, the current low interest rates, and the and proven prudent leadership of XYZ senior management that has positioned the company as one of the most efficient and profitable cement producers, our agreement to arrange a $10 million Term Loan Bond for company expansion will provide minimal risks to investors.

Procedural Report Example

SETTING GOALS: A GUIDE FOR MANAGERS

INTRODUCTION

In a survey conducted last month among managers, a majority (89 percent) expressed concern about the difficulties of setting, measuring, and achieving goals related to both personal and corporate performance. In response to this need, senior management sought the advice of several experts and consultants to address this issue. The following suggestions highlight their major points and observations about how managers can set and meet goals as individuals and as members of a larger corporate entity.

SELECTING THE RIGHT GOALS

Just as an organization must carefully select the goals most beneficial to yearly health and growth, so too must its managers focus their energies on goals most essential to particular needs and special skills. By focusing their efforts and resources on selected rather than on numerous goals, managers can significantly increase their chances of success. On a larger scale, these efforts can affect and enhance corporate vitality and stability. The most pressing question for most managers, of course, will be: "How do I determine what are the best goals?" One solution is to prepare a checklist of alternative goals and then ask the following questions:

1. What do I want to accomplish in the next six to 12 months?
2. Which goals warrant priority and why?
3. Which goals would senior management like to see me accomplish?
4. How do the goals affect my staff's workload?
5. What do I do best? In what areas are my skills most useful and productive?
6. What weaker areas must I strengthen?
7. How will these goals contribute to my department and organization at large?
8. Do I have a plan?
9. Do my goals duplicate or conflict with the goals of others or with corporate policy?
10. Are my goals realistic?
11. Can I set a tentative completion date?
12. How can I evaluate the long-range benefits of achieving of my goals?

PREPARING A PLAN

Once the goals have been set and the above questions have been carefully considered, the next step is to devise a plan for implementing and evaluating the goals. This is best accomplished by focusing on specific rather than on general concerns. In expressing the scope of the goals in a statement, it's important to concentrate on the particulars. For example:

GOAL: To develop a training program by August 19 after identifying employee needs, interests, staff requirements, and delivery formats. Had this idea been expressed more generally ("To develop a training program") the specific tasks would not be immediately identified, and time would be lost as the manager sorted out the specifics of what he or she wanted to accomplish. It is not until the tasks and stages are recognized that the manager can assign components to staff members. The manager then must set a completion date for each task and schedule periodic review meetings.

REVIEWING THE GOALS

Because goals set early in the year can prove secondary to others as time passes and needs change, the manager should carefully and systematically review goals in terms of relevance and probable achievement. No goal should be pursued merely for its own sake or to satisfy the need to complete a project. Goals that may prove counterproductive to ongoing individual and corporate needs should be discarded, especially if they are judged outdated and no longer viable.

CONCLUSION

Setting clear goals offers managers the opportunity to accomplish particular aims, focus on long-range issues of concern, and invariably leads to more effective time management. The ability to set and achieve selected goals is ultimately crucial to effective daily and long range job performance and productivity.

12

Instructions, Presentations, Proposals, and Resumes

"How do I know what I think until I see what I say?"
—E. M. Forster

Instructions

OUR DAILY AND PROFESSIONAL LIVES are filled with instructions. There are instructions for using a power tool, installing the latest software, operating a cell phone, cooking dinner, installing a new sink, programming your VCR, and assembling your child's bicycle, not to mention instructions from your spouse about what not to say in front of your in-laws. In business, your job might involve providing payment instructions for customers, shipping procedures for vendors, using new software, adhering to hiring policies, completing questionnaires, or submitting proposals.

Who among us hasn't tossed a set of instructions aside after uttering, "These instructions are useless!" On the other hand, you may know the story of the help-desk advisor who received a phone call from a customer explaining that the new computer she bought was not working properly. She went on to say that the image on her monitor was frozen. She added her manual "said to press any key," but she did not know which one was the "any" key. Absurd? Comical? Yes and no. If there is one occasion for Murphy's Law to exert its force on writing, it's when anyone tries to write instructions. Think of all the times you had to explain once, twice, maybe three times what appeared to you to be the simplest task. When trying to explain technical instructions to a nontechnical reader, the opportunities for confusion increase a thousand percent. You try saying it another way. You draw a picture. You write the instructions in simple terms. You actually show your listener how to do something. In writing you can't do that because you are usually not there to explain what step to take or procedure to follow if a problem occurs.

Writing instructions is never easy for a number of reasons. The first and most significant has to do with your knowledge of the subject. Usually the more you know and even the more adept you are at your subject, the more difficulty you have writing clear instructions. When you perform a process often or routinely many of the procedures become second nature to you. You follow each step automatically. In writing, these same steps occur in your mind but are often not expressed for your readers.

For example, let's say you have to write instructions for changing a tire on a deserted highway. There are no public telephones and you do not have a cell phone to call your local road service. In most instances, you would most likely either forget to tell your reader to first shut off the engine or how to use the jack or take the spare out of the trunk or loosen the bolts. At times your readers will also need to know what purpose the instructions will serve. They will also need to know what not to do: "Warning: Do not connect the wires when standing in a pool of water."

The next obstacles to writing instructions are clarity and simplicity. Instructions are not the occasion for showing off your writing skills. Use simple words and sentences. Prefer active to passive voice—that is, place your activity words in the beginning.

NOT: The screw is turned three times to the right.

BUT: Turn the screw three times to the right.

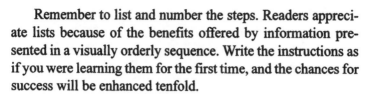

Remember to list and number the steps. Readers appreciate lists because of the benefits offered by information presented in a visually orderly sequence. Write the instructions as if you were learning them for the first time, and the chances for success will be enhanced tenfold.

Here are words and phrases you will find helpful when writing instructions:

always	connect	installation	procedures
avoid	described	method	remove
caution	explain	normal	standard steps
change	how to	note	usually
check	indicated	operation	warning

Example

Choosing a Location for Your Fax Machine

1. Place your fax machine on a flat, stable surface, such as a desk or table.
2. Select a place that is free of vibration and shocks.
3. Locate the machine near a telephone jack and a standard, grounded power outlet.
4. Do not place the machine near heaters, air conditioners, water, chemicals, or refrigerators.
5. Do not expose the machine to direct sunlight, excessive heat, moisture, or dust.
6. Do not connect the machine to electrical outlets controlled by wall switches or automatic timers.

Presentations

"Speak briefly, and to the point."

—Cato

At first glance, the most noticeable difference between oral and written communication is in the manner of presentation, spoken versus written words. As a result, the subtle distinctions between the two modes of communication may not be immediately apparent. Both methods provide information in the form of facts, opinions, judgments, numerical data, conclusions, and recommendations. Both require similar tasks during preparation:

1. The purpose and scope of the report must be identified.
2. The audience must be analyzed or considered.
3. Illustrations may be employed, though more so in oral presentations.
4. The tone must be appropriate to both subject and occasion.

On closer examination, however, it becomes apparent that there are advantages and differences unique to both oral and written communication. As a tangible document composed of so many pages, the written report conveys a concreteness and permanence that underscores its importance. Even though the reader can scan the report at a leisurely pace, the reading process requires active participation. Certain passages can be highlighted, commented upon, or reread.

The oral report or presentation, by contrast, allows the speaker to verbally emphasize major points through vocal tone, inflection, volume, and well-timed pauses. Ideas can be explained, clarified, or exemplified. There is greater flexibility in matters of usage and grammatical correctness because listeners don't always expect public speakers to be letter-perfect. The speaker can use body language and facial expressions to emphasize key ideas or even influence the listener's response. Humor can be injected depending on the topic.

Planning the Presentation

Similar to a written report, an oral presentation requires careful planning. Important facts to consider include the scope, purpose, and focus as well as formats for organizing and developing ideas and findings. Here are some points to bear in mind when devising a first draft:

- Avoid discussing difficult and complex issues in excessive detail.
- Limit the use of facts and numerical data to supporting key ideas and findings.
- Present the most important ideas and issues in the opening or closing.
- Summarize main ideas in concluding comments.
- Prefer familiar words to enhance a conversational tone.
- Prepare answers to possible questions.

Considering the Audience

The need to consider your audience is no less important for an oral presentation than it is for a written one. The same questions must be posed in terms of the audience's general background, interest in the subject, and ability to understand any complex or technical material. You need to decide if the presentation will be informal or formal. Should you include an anecdote or two or perhaps some humor here and there or be strictly limited to sober facts? How long can you expect the audience to listen to the topic? How much detail will they appreciate? Should you allow for a question and answer period and if so, then for how long? Whenever we speak we are our most attentive listener. Can we expect the same of our audience? Perhaps not. For this reason you would do well to assume the listener's chair and ask these questions:

1. If I had to attend my presentation, how would I prefer the material to be presented? Informally? With humor? Lots of illustrations? Brevity?
2. What would hold my attention throughout the presentation? A variety of topics? Benefits to me? Pitfalls to avoid? Hard-earned lessons?
3. Considering the subject matter, would there be a time in the presentation when my mind is likely to wander? What would keep me interested?

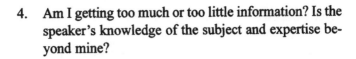

4. Am I getting too much or too little information? Is the speaker's knowledge of the subject and expertise beyond mine?

Preparing an Outline

For many speakers, the greatest fear is that at some crucial moment in the discussion their minds will go blank or they will embarrassingly stutter and stumble from one incohesive thought to another. Preparing an outline of key ideas will help reduce such anxiety. Reducing longer sentences and masses of data to key words or phrases will serve as "touchstones" to memory and continuity of thought.

For instance, if your sentence reads:

The School of Business Education serves approximately 1,500 students, of which 60 percent are undergraduate and 40 percent graduate students, and employs a full-time faculty of 30 instructors.

In your outline you would note:

*   School of Business Education: 1,500 students.
*   60% undergraduate; 40% graduate.
*   30 full-time faculty.

Much easier to remember, isn't it? Preparing an outline consisting of key phrases and the sequence of information can help you feel a lot less pressure and convey a smoother flow of information.

Writing the Opening

There is no guaranteed way to attract your audience's attention during the opening moments of your presentation. However, if your listeners are not "hooked" in the beginning, there is little chance of their coming round afterwards, unless you resort to slides or other illustrations. There are a number of proven initial techniques you can use to help you get your audience involved. For example:

Offer Interesting or Unsettling Facts

Sometimes unusual or controversial information can "jump start" your discussion. You don't have to make melodramatic announcements or sensational claims. Rather, you can relate a little known fact or correct a mistaken notion:

> It is hard to believe that despite the enormous educational opportunities in the United States, there are more than 40 million functionally illiterate Americans. Even more startling, half of the poor souls are high school graduates.

Involve the Listener

All salespeople know that before they can hope to close a sale they must gain their customer's attention. There must be some involvement or shared understanding. Asking a question such as this will help diffuse any boredom or indifference to your topic:

> What can we do about this problem that is certain to undermine our political and economical stability and growth in the coming decade?

Use a Quotation

Quotations are wonderful aids to initiating, developing and concluding your discussion. Remember that quotes should neither be too long nor complicated.

> *"There is only one thing in the world worse than being talked about, and that is not being talked about."*
> —Oscar Wilde

> *"There was things which he stretched, but mainly he told the truth."*
> —Mark Twain

Relate an Anecdote

Most people love stories and anecdotes, so you might want to tell an amusing tale that aptly serves to introduce your subject. Anecdotes should never be long nor contain objectionable material or words. Rather, relevance and good taste are the best guidelines to appropriateness. Here is one way to introduce a report on functional illiteracy:

> The other day the computerized cash register at my local supermarket broke down after totaling the price of a gallon of milk, loaf of bread, and dog biscuits to $6.37. Since the drawer was open, I handed a $20 bill to the cashier fully expecting she would be able to make change. She stared at the total amount due. Then she stared at the $20 bill. Then she stared at me. "I have to wait until the register comes back on," she announced.
>
> My experience is not unique. Are we over-relying on machines to help us carry out previously simple tasks or facing a crisis of functional illiteracy? I'd like to share my findings with you today in discussing the state of basic skills in the U.S. workforce.

Provide Background Information

Background details provide the listener with a frame of reference for your discussion. Very often this information can include definitions of important terms, a statement of purpose or your goals, and any additional insights that may help your listener fully appreciate your comments. Keep the number of details to a minimum to avoid your listener experiencing information overload. The benefit of providing background details rests in orienting your listeners to your presentation's focus and scope, not merely overwhelming them with endless facts and figures. Here's an example:

> Last year, 35 percent of the corporations surveyed for this report repeated the equivalent of high school basic level reading, writing, and math skills for their employees. One major firm spent 5 million dollars to train 14,000 workers nationwide. What are the reasons for this crisis in basic skills among members of the American workforce? Too much television? Too many video games? Are there solutions to this growing problem?

Concluding the Presentation

If the opening remarks of your presentation must attract your audience's attention and your subsequent comments develop and sustain that interest and attention, the conclusion will either reinforce key points and findings or urge action or further involvement. No information should be introduced in your conclusion that has not been previously discussed. Also, in most instances, a simple "thank you" is the best postscript.

Don't Read the Report!

In Shakespeare's *Hamlet,* when a group of actors visits Elsinore Castle, Hamlet advises them to "suit the action to the word, the word to the action." The same advice holds true today. Although you need not be an actor to deliver an effective presentation, you must consider a tone and style appropriate to the report's content and audience. Using a light and breezy manner in announcing poor earnings performance or loss of sizable contracts will hardly be appreciated by your listeners. Nor would an emotionless, monosyllabic droning delivery convey a humorous anecdote.

Any speaker who simply reads a presentation in a monotone voice is certain to lose the audience's attention. Remember to convey a sense of enthusiasm no matter how dry the topic. Just as no one enjoys one-sided conversations with people who either only talk about themselves or monopolize a discussion, neither will your listeners enjoy your endless stream of thoughts. We rarely appreciate anyone talking *at* rather than *to* us.

At the same time, reading a report is not conversation. The rhythms of speech are different, more measured and pronounced. We don't want to have many extended moments of silence between sentences. The tone must convey liveliness but not shouting. Your audience is not expecting a sermon. They can get that elsewhere. People want information expressed in a manner they can enjoy and understand. They want to feel that

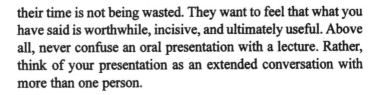

their time is not being wasted. They want to feel that what you have said is worthwhile, incisive, and ultimately useful. Above all, never confuse an oral presentation with a lecture. Rather, think of your presentation as an extended conversation with more than one person.

Proposals

Proposals are detailed documents designed to persuade your reader to accept an idea, recommendation, or solution to a problem, adopt a plan, buy a product, use your services, or give you money for research. Proposals are sometimes written to offer suggestions. Proposals can take many forms. Depending on the content and your relationship to the reader, they can be informal or formal, brief or lengthy, and expressed through memos, letters, as separate formal documents, or perhaps even via e-mail. They can be written for internal or external audiences, may be solicited or unsolicited, or may be in response to a Request for a Proposal (commonly referred to as an RFP) or a Request for a Quote (RFQ).

Strategy Suggestions for Successful Proposals

Whether the goal is to persuade upper management to accept your suggestions for improving productivity or for your consulting group to win a sizable government contract, think of your proposal as a variation of a sales letter. After all, isn't the basic idea of any proposal, including one for marriage, to "sell" your reader (or prospective mate) to accept your ideas or you? In all proposals, written or verbal, the overall thrust and tone must be persuasive. Moreover, similar to a marriage proposal, you will need to supply supporting details, such as facts, statistics, numerical data, approach or procedures, criteria or standards for evaluating effectiveness or success, fees, sequences of activities, dates, and lists of personnel or who will be invited to the wedding. Most importantlt, your proposal must include a benefit statement or list of benefits. What do you hope to accomplish? How will your proposal save the company time and money? What solutions are you offering that will assuredly address an ongoing problem? In brief, what's in it for your reader? Every successful salesperson knows that the best way to get the order is to offer potential customers exactly what they need and want. I have known imaginative sales representatives who were effective at creating a need for their customers or leading them toward seeing a need they didn't know existed.

Perhaps the best method for emphasizing the benefits of your proposal is to place them in a cover letter or the introduction. The advantages to your reader must be clearly stated. They must be able to see *how* you can save them time and money, improve workplace safety, increase productivity and job performance, enhance a product or service, or provide needed training. In between, the details should realistically and logically support your premise. Solutions must seem practical and feasible. Arguments must be irrefutable and based on fact. Weigh all factors before offering a conclusive solution or recommendation. Emphasize the likelihood of immediate practical application or advantage. Consider and possibly address opposing viewpoints or alternative approaches. Perhaps ask these questions: How convincing is my proposal? Would I accept it? Would I feel comfortable presenting it to upper management or allocating considerable funds in accepting the proposal?

When responding to an RFP, review carefully all instructions and wherever possible rework and include any particular buzzwords or jargon in your sentences. If possible, contact the agency or individual with authority to approve the proposal to clarify any confusing guidelines. Address all issues and questions. Avoid evasive or vague responses and comments. Perhaps it's best if you think of writing and submitting proposals as similar to playing a game where you have only one chance to succeed. To paraphrase F. Scott Fitzgerald's observation: There are no second acts in submitting proposals.

Designing/Formatting Proposals

There is no one way to design and structure a proposal. If you're responding to a Request for a Proposal, you will have to adhere to the guidelines outlined. Sometimes a proposal consists of preprinted pages consisting of a series of numbered or lettered headings followed by blank spaces. However the instructions are presented, you must follow them to the letter. Do not attempt to be creative or imaginatively improve the format. To do so is to risk having your proposal rejected for "noncompliance" to strict guidelines. (I know because it has happened to me.) Formal proposals often include the following elements:

1. Cover letter.
2. Title page.
3. Introduction discussing the subject.
4. Scope of work.
5. Background.
6. Statement of objectives.
7. Strategy, work plan, or approach.
8. List of materials or equipment.
9. Schedule of work or activities.
10. Professional qualifications and experience.
11. List of personnel.
12. Evaluative methods.
13. Budget (costs/fees).
14. Conclusion.
15. Appendix of supporting documents.

Resumes

Everyone who has to work for a living strives to get a "good" or "better" job, which for most people consists of daily activities that are interesting and satisfying and that fully utilize their skills and experience. Some people want a job that offers challenges. Some enjoy travel and being outdoors. Others prefer a job that allows them to work on their own. Everyone wants a job that offers a decent salary, fringe benefits, retirement programs, and pleasant working conditions. Yet whether working toward obtaining a good job or an ideal one, your success in achieving that goal ultimately depends on your ability to "sell" yourself on paper, which consists of a letter of application and a resume, or detailed summary of your education, skills, and job experience.

Would *You* Hire You?

Perhaps the first question you need to ask when preparing a resume is this: Would you hire you? This question will prompt you to engage is helpful self-analysis of your strengths and weaknesses. For example:

- What job-related skills or training do you have to offer your employer?
- How much experience do you have in a particular field?
- What are your long-term professional goals?
- Do you possess any unique skills, such as speaking two languages, that would prove helpful in your daily responsibilities?
- Have you developed any special technical or expertise that will enhance your appeal to your prospective employer?
- Have you had exceptional job experiences that will prove valuable to your job performance?
- What particular accomplishments have you achieved that are relevant to the job you are seeking or reveal a positive character trait?
- What don't you want in a job?
- Are there limitations or constraints, such as relocating to another state or salary requirements?
- What qualities, skills, knowledge, and interests will enable you to contribute to a company?

Letter of Application

If we are what we write to those who have never met us, then both your letter of application and resume will demonstrate your ability to communicate clearly and to the point. Because the letter of application is your initial sales pitch, you need to impress your reader not with just a list of details but also your writing skills. Your letter of application will reveal to your potential employer not merely what you know or have accomplished but your ability (or inability) to express your thoughts on paper. The next time you glance at your local newspaper's job section, notice how many jobs ads require that applicants have "excellent written and verbal communication skills." Include the following information in your letter of application:

1. **The specific job for which you are applying.** Incorporate as much wording as possible from the job announcement or briefly describe the type of position you are seeking.

2. **Your reasons for applying,** such as seeking greater professional challenges or utilizing of job skills and professional expertise.

3. **How you can contribute to the organization.** List the benefits the company will obtain by hiring you. Mention the special skills or significant experience and skills you can offer. Do not offer comments regarding your desire for higher pay, shorter working hours, and the chance to work with people who will like you.

4. **Degrees, professional licenses, and certifications.** Use a traditional letter format. Begin the letter with "Dear Mr. or Ms. _____" if you have a specific name (even if you feel uncomfortable doing so in addressing a stranger). If applying to a post office box number or you do not know the gender of the reader, use "Dear Sir or Madam," "Dear Human Resource Manager," or "Dear Personnel Representative" in your salutation. Always close with "Sincerely" or "Yours truly."

Job Application Cover Letter Example

June 3, 20—
Alexis Smythe, Managing Editor
Company Name
Address
City, State Zip

Dear Ms. Smythe:

In response to the editorial position advertised in yesterday's *New York Times*, enclosed is my resume, which outlines my considerable experience as an editor for various technical publications.

Although I have thoroughly enjoyed my current position as a senior editor of the popular *Love That Technology*, I am currently seeking greater challenges and opportunities for my skills.

My ten years of general editorial experience includes a working knowledge of the business aspects of publishing technical magazines and professional journals that would enable me to make an added contribution to your publication. When I attended Georgia State University and majored in English and journalism, I edited the college newspaper for three years. Many thanks for considering my application. I look forward to hearing from you.

Sincerely,

Writing the Resume

Various structural formats lend themselves to resume design, but the one you choose must be readable. Because your readers will have dozens of resumes to review, you need to present yourself in the most concise and visually appealing manner. Therefore, remember to present information about your professional experience selectively. You don't have to list every job, award, and accomplishment, only what will prove appropriate to the position you hope to obtain. If possible, avoid mentioning salary expectations in the resume. Wait until you've been invited for an interview (and then only near

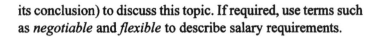

its conclusion) to discuss this topic. If required, use terms such as *negotiable* and *flexible* to describe salary requirements.

Format for a Traditional Resume

A traditional resume contains the following information:

- Name.
- Contact Information: address, telephone number, and e-mail address.

 Sample Resume

Jeremy Mutsey
715 Laguna Lane
Los Angeles, CA 90048
jmutsey@isp.com

Objective: *A challenging, responsible executive position in hotel management.*

Experience:

- General manager of a large hotel in southern California.
- Responsible for overall operations that include:
    - Coordinating various social functions.
    - Evaluating personnel performance.
    - Scheduling training sessions for all service personnel.

Employment History:

1997–present: General Manager, Beverly Hills Palace

1992–1997: Catering Manager, Hilton Hotel, Chicago

1988–1992: Manager, Gandy's Restaurant, New York

Education:

B.S. Hotel Management, New York University

Franklin K. Lane High School

References: Available upon request.

- Objective: Your career goals or reason for applying for the position.
- Experience: List first the most appropriate job-related experience.
- Employment History: Begin with the most recent or current position. Include dates and responsibilities.
- Education: List according to highest degree obtained.
- Additional Qualifications.
- References: State that these are available upon request.

Action Verbs

When describing your accomplishments and experience, use the action words below to achieve for greater force and precision. Here are some examples:

accomplished	created	operated
administered	designed	organized
arranged	developed	planned
conducted	devised	researched
constructed	implemented	supervised
contributed	initiated	
coordinated	managed	

Proofreading and Editing

Your reader will judge your application and resume on its correctness. Any glaring errors will stand out as if underlined in red. You don't want to shoot yourself in the foot, so to speak, the way these applicants did:

I work with 20 odd people.
One of my strengths is my accuricy.

Proofread for spelling (don't trust the spell-checker entirely), subject and verb agreement, punctuation, capitalization, dates, and general correct usage. Do not use slang.

Stretching the Truth

In our time of Internet information access, don't attempt to exaggerate the truth of the details you provide regarding your education, work experience, current salary level, publications, awards, and any other feature that you believe will enhance your appeal to a prospective employer. Thanks to modern technology and the information detection it offers, you won't be able to fool even some of the people anytime. It's one thing to embellish an accomplishment or two and another to lie outright and be discovered. Stretching the truth beyond the proverbial "shadow of a doubt" may only ultimately serve to tighten the noose around your neck. If it's discovered after you've been hired, aside from the embarrassment and humiliation you will experience, you will either be fired immediately or be so discredited you will have no choice but to resign. Embellishing a bit will not prove harmful. At the same time, remember that you do not have to be overly modest in presenting yourself. Listing accomplishments you are proud of will often reflect additional skills and may well impress your reader enough to invite you for an interview.

Appendices

Business Letter Models

Thank-You/Appreciation

Purpose

To express appreciation or to acknowledge assistance.

Tone

Cordial and sincere.

Content Guidelines/Format

1. Thank the reader for any assistance or contributions.
2. Mention the specific reasons for your appreciation or value of the reader's efforts or contributions.
3. Close with "Sincerely."

Helpful Words

appreciate	lovely
beautiful	memorable
charming	tasteful
delightful	thoughtful
generous	useful
kind	valuable

Example

January 10, 20—

Dear Joan:

I very much appreciate your help in providing information essential to the success of our obtaining the Lazzo account. The data you compiled was an important factor in Lazzo senior management's favorable decision toward our company.

Sincerely,

Congratulations

Purpose

To offer congratulations for a personal or professional accomplishment.

Tone

Enthusiastic and sincere.

Content Guidelines/Format

1. Express congratulations.

2. Mention your appreciation or awareness of the skills, qualities, or efforts that were essential to the reader's accomplishment or that underlie the special occasion (marriage, promotion).

3. Close cordially with "Sincerely" or "Best regards."

Helpful Words

accomplishment	honor	remarkable
achievement	impressive	superb
distinguished	outstanding	unique
exceptional	peerless	well-deserved

Example

February 20, 20—

Dear Frank:

    I am so pleased to learn of your promotion to Director of Marketing. I believe no one is more qualified or deserving of this position. Congratulations.

Best regards,

Welcome

Purpose

    To issue welcome to new employees or members of an organization.

Tone

    Personal and sincere.

Content Guidelines/Format

1. Extend welcome in the first sentence.
2. State how the reader's background/experience/ knowledge will contribute to your organization.
3. Offer assistance if necessary.
4. Close with "Cordially."

Helpful Words

assistance	happy
delighted	pleased
excited	support
glad	welcome

Example

June 24, 20—

Dear Ms. Jensen:

On behalf of the West End Garden Association I want to extend to you a warm welcome to our club. Your reputation for growing prize-winning roses does our association great honor to include you among its notable members. No doubt your expertise will be most sought after.

Please let me know of any needs you may have.

Cordially,

Invitation to an Event

Purpose

To extend an invitation.

Tone

Appropriate to the occasion.

Content Guidelines/Format

1. Name the individual or organization issuing invitation.
2. Describe the purpose of the event or occasion.
3. List the time, date, location, and attire.
4. Close cordially, expressing hope that the reader will be able to accept the invitation.

Helpful Words

accept	event
attend	honor
celebrate	invite
commemorate	salute

Example

July 15, 20—

Dear Mrs. Fabrizzi:

Our board of directors has asked me to invite you to speak at our National Conference of Poker Players, to be held in Las Vegas on October 28. All travel and hotel expenses will be provided. We would be able to pay you an honorarium of $500 as well. I look forward to hearing that you will be able to join us.

Yours truly,

Invitation to Apply for Credit

Purpose

To invite potential customers to apply for credit.

Tone

Friendly, enthusiastic, and positive.

Content Guidelines/Format

1. Describe the nature of your business or organization.
2. Stress the advantages and convenience of opening a credit account.
3. Invite the reader to complete and sign the enclosed application form. Ensure confidentiality.
4. Urge immediate response by providing a postage-free mailer, toll-free telephone number, e-mail address, Web site, or fax number.
5. Close with urge to act.

Helpful Words

advantage	approve	credit	extend
application	benefit	creditworthy	finance
apply	convenience	excellent	history

increase	loan	record	verify
information	pre-approved	report	
limit	preferred	submit	

Example

August 19, 20—

Dear Martha Grace:

Because we value the way you've managed your Impress Credit account, we are pleased to offer you the opportunity to upgrade to the Gold card level. Your Gold card will provide you with these benefits:

- Increased buying power.
- Auto rental insurance.
- Travel and emergency assistance.
- Emergency case disbursement.
- Greater peace of mind.

Reply today by completing and returning the attached form or call toll free 1-800-123-4567.

We hope you will take this opportunity to enjoy additional credit and prestige with your Gold Impress card.

Sincerely,

Credit/Loan Approval

Purpose

To inform reader his/her application for credit or a loan has been approved.

Tone

Enthusiastic.

Content Guidelines/Format

1. Announce that credit or loan approval has been granted.

2. Congratulate the reader.
3. Specify the terms and limits.
4. Remind the reader of the importance of maintaining credit standing and timely payments.
5. Provide a phone number for assistance or questions and close cordially.

Helpful Words

advantage	credit	increase	record
application	creditworthy	information	report
apply	excellent	limit	submit
approve	extend	loan	verify
benefit	finance	pre-approved	
convenience	history	preferred	

Example

January 4, 20—

Dear Mr. Racoonia:

Enclosed is your new Gold Impress card, which we approve for only our most creditworthy customers. Please note the one-time fee of $95.00 will appear on your first statement, which you will receive before January 15. Please remember all payments are due no later than the date listed on your statement. If you have any questions or need assistance, please call our 24-hour customer service desk at 1-800-123-4567.

Sincerely,

Credit Refusal

Purpose

To inform the reader that his/her application for credit is denied.

Tone

Courteous, direct, and sincere.

Content Guidelines/Format

1. Thank the reader for applying for credit or loan.
2. State politely that credit cannot be approved.
3. List specific reasons for the decision.
4. Invite the reader to apply again at a later date.
5. Close with "Cordially."

Helpful Words

credit	late	overdue	review
collection	limit	owe	unpaid
debt	past due	regretfully	
history	pattern	report	

Example

March 15, 20—

Dear Mr. Higgenbottom:

Upon careful review of your recent application, we are sorry to report we are unable to approve an increase in credit. Our decision is based on your refusal to supply current employment information. Should you decide to submit details of your employment at a later date, we will be happy to review another application.

Cordially,

Collection

Purpose

To remind the reader that payment on his/her account is overdue.

Tone

Polite but firm.

Content Guidelines/Format

1. Remind the reader that payment is past due.
2. Urge payment upon receipt of letter.
3. Provide a phone number to discuss making payment arrangements or problems.
4. Close with urge to respond.

Helpful Words

action	concerned	past due	resolve
advise	default	prompt	settle
arrears	invoice	records	unpaid
avoid	oversight	remainder	urge
balance	neglect	remit	
bill	nonpayment	repay	

Example

February 14, 20—

Dear Mrs. Twelvetrees:

Your payment for the 10 bird cages you purchased last December is now 90 days past due. Because you are a long-time customer, having bought dozens of birds from us, it is with great reluctance that we send you this letter. I remember your mentioning your plans to travel sometime in January to the Amazon jungle in order to observe one of the rarest species of parrots. I hope you had an enjoyable trip and look forward to hearing of your experiences when you next visit our store. In the meantime, I must ask that you send a check upon receipt of this letter to my attention so I may clear your account.

Sincerely,

Sales or Promotion

Purpose

To encourage or persuade the reader to purchase a product or subscribe to a service.

Tone

Enthusiastic.

Content Guidelines/Format

1. Describe the product or service.
2. Create interest by specifying how the product or service will benefit the reader/organization.
3. List features and advantages over competition.
4. Urge immediate action or response through a toll-free telephone number, e-mail address, fax number, or Web site.

Helpful Words

advantages	easy	innovative	simple
affordable	economical	labor-saving	strong
attractive	effective	new	time-saving
benefit	efficient	powerful	useful
comfortable	exclusive	practical	valuable
dependable	extensive	profitable	warrantee
durable	guaranteed	revolutionizing	

Example

November 10, 20—

Dear Ms. Richards:

How often do you wish you could say exactly what you truly feel the next time someone at work or home passes a nasty comment or insults you outright? Do you work with extremely difficult people, often irritable and impossible to please, always finding fault with everything you do and critical of all your efforts? Do you have to report to a supervisor who cannot resist uttering negative comments about your job performance and productivity? Do you have that in-law who can never resist telling you that color is not for you or your hair looks terrible lately?

We are not born assertive; we must learn it. We must learn to say, "This far and no farther" to those who take advantage of our generous natures and mistake kindness and agreeability for weakness. In one day you can learn how to verbally "defend" yourself from any difficult person you may encounter, whether a surly coworker or snide, indifferent clerk at your local motor vehicle bureau.

Take the first step to becoming assertive. Simply mail the enclosed registration card today or call the toll-free number to enroll in our popular workshop, "Assertive Training for Dealing With Difficult People," which will be held in glittering Las Vegas. Start taking control of your life. Right now!

Sincerely,

Refusal

Purpose

To refuse a proposal, offer, or service.

Tone

Polite but firm.

Content Guidelines/Format

1. Specify the subject of refusal.
2. State the specific reasons.
3. List acceptable conditions or changes that may lead you to reconsider the offer/proposal.
4. Diffuse disappointment by thanking the reader for interest, suggestion, concern, or offer.

Helpful Words

cancel	limits	reject	unavailable
cannot	prevents	return	unfavorable
decline	refuse	sorry	unfortunately
difficult	regret	unable	

Example

May 12, 20—

Dear Mr. Allworthy:

Thank you very much for sending me an invitation to your forthcoming lecture, "The Use of the Comma in Shakespeare's Plays." I have attended a number of your lectures and have always found the content informative and your presentation no less than spellbinding. Although any of your future lectures would no doubt be of interest to me, I am afraid that a prior speaking engagement of my own prevents me from attending yours in June.

Yours truly,

Transmittal

Purpose

To provide information regarding the content of a report, proposal, manual, procedures, contract, and so on.

Tone

Informal and direct.

Content Guidelines/Format

1. State the title of the document.
2. Summarize key features, details, accomplishments, limitations or special considerations, problems, conclusions, and recommendations.
3. Express appreciation to anyone who assisted in preparing the document.

4. Express hope that the reader will find the information helpful and informative.
5. Close with "Sincerely" or "Regards."

Helpful Words

announce	guidelines	policy	proposal
attached	outline	procedure	report
enclosed	plans	program	statement

Example

October 29, 20—

Dear Jules:

Enclosed is a copy of my screenplay, *Teenage Werewolves from Outer Space*, for your review. During lunch last week you mentioned that you believed demand among the various studios would be very intense for this script. I made the changes you requested and agree that the story is now tighter and the plot more realistic. I also adjusted the villainous characters to less resemble the studio executives you suggested would be apparent to anyone in the movie business. I hope you agree we have a potential winner here.

Regards,

Introducing or Outlining a Policy or Procedure

Purpose

To explain a current or revised policy or procedure.

Tone

Simple and direct.

Content Guidelines/Format

1. State the name of the policy or procedure.

2. Note the advantages, goals, or reasons.
3. List the key features or steps.
4. Note the effective date if new or revised policy/procedure.
5. Offer assistance for questions or concerns.

Helpful Words

guidelines	method	requirements	techniques
instructions	procedures	steps	

Example

July 28, 20—

Dear Ms. Hadley:

Please follow these procedures for submitting training requests for your staff:

1. Submit a brief statement to my office describing the need and relevance of the specific training to the prospective participants' needs.
2. Describe the benefits of the training in terms of individual needs, practical application, professional growth, job requirements, and ability to improve performance and productivity.
3. Schedule no more than three individuals from the same department to attend a training program on the same day.

Please call Donna May at ext. 125 for additional information.

Sincerely,

Reference or Recommendation

Purpose

To offer a positive evaluation of an individual's experience, qualifications, background, character, and prospects for success regarding a job application or promotion.

Tone

Professional, direct, and cordial.

Content Guidelines/Format

1. Describe your relationship with and knowledge of the applicant's experience and background.
2. Specify your understanding of the candidate's current responsibilities, skills, performance, productivity, and personal attributes.
3. Offer examples of the candidate's achievements and contributions to your organization.
4. Cite potential for success in future positions.
5. Offer to provide additional information if requested. List phone number or e-mail address.
6. Close with "Sincerely."

Helpful Words

admirable	dependable	helpful	professional
capable	effective	honest	reliable
commendable	efficient	honorable	resourceful
competent	ethical	invaluable	responsible
conscientious	excellent	inventive	self-starter
considerate	friendly	loyal	
cooperative	hard-working	productive	

Example

April 20, 20—

Dear Mr. David:

I have known Carol Johnson for three years. She has been an invaluable member of my staff and has contributed greatly to the effectiveness of my department. Patricia's energy, enthusiasm for her work, diligent attention to her responsibilities, resourcefulness, maturity of judgment, and all-around good nature have made her an asset to our company. I understand that Carol is seeking greater challenges for her skills. I recommend her most highly and without reservation to the management position available with your organization.

Sincerely,

Inquiry

Purpose

To request information.

Tone

Cordial.

Content Guidelines/Format

1. Introduce yourself and list your job title or job responsibilities.
2. State specifically your request and reasons/need for the information requested.
3. Specify the date when the information is needed.
4. Enclose a postage-free envelope, e-mail address, or fax number.
5. Express appreciation for any information the recipient may be able to provide.

Helpful Words

able	guidance	permission	refer
appreciate	help	possible	reply
assistance	information	prompt	request
cooperation	inquiry	question	urgent
give	obtain	recommend	willing

Example

June 15, 20—

Dear Ms. Diaz:

I am very interested in learning about the various seminars your company offers for on-site presentation. I am responsible for overseeing a staff of 25 accountants who are highly competent employees. However, the level of their interpersonal communication skills needs to be raised to allow them to effectively interact with our various clients.

One of the managers in another department recently attended one of your presentation skills seminars and found it helpful. He suggested I contact your company for a list of workshops you would offer at our headquarters here in San Francisco. I would appreciate your sending information at your earliest convenience. Also, do you offer group discount rates?

Sincerely,

Reply to a Letter of Inquiry

Purpose

To acknowledge receipt of letter of inquiry and provide information.

Tone

Courteous and direct.

Content Guidelines/Format

1. Express your pleasure in providing the information requested.
2. Provide complete details and answers.
3. If unable to provide any information, list the reasons.
4. Offer further assistance if necessary.
5. Close with "Sincerely."

Helpful Words

able	help	prompt	suggest
appreciate	information	question	urgent
assistance	inquiry	recommend	willing
cooperation	obtain	refer	
give	permission	reply	
guidance	possible	request	

Example

June 18, 20–

Dear Mr. Davis:

Enclosed is a catalog of our various seminars, all of which are available for on-site presentation. Considering the training needs you mentioned in your letter of June 15, our two-day workshop "Successful Interpersonal Skills" is most apt to meet your training needs. The workshop, along with several others that address related training issues, is described on pages 7–10. One of our customer-service representatives will be happy to provide you with additional information regarding the workshop content and format and discount fees available to groups of 20 or more. Please call our toll-free number or contact us at *www.training.org*.

Sincerely,

Negative Response to a Letter of Inquiry

Purpose

To refuse a request for information.

Tone

Courteous but firm.

Content Guidelines/Format

1. Express your appreciation for the request.

2. Provide the reasons for not granting the request.
3. Offer to help in another way or suggest another source of information.
4. Close with "Sincerely."

Helpful Words

cannot	policy	rules	unavailable
decline	problem	sorry	unfortunately
guidelines	procedure	turn down	
limited	regretfully	unable	

Example

January 7, 20—

Dear Mr. Ugarty:

Thank you for your recent inquiry regarding our new line of underwater digital cameras.

I also read the *Times* article that briefly mentioned them and can well understand your interest in learning more about what the writer believes will prove a revolutionary camera. Unfortunately, because these cameras are still in the developmental phase, information is unavailable to the public at this time. I do, however, appreciate your interest in our forthcoming products.

Sincerely,

Acknowledgment or Agreement

Purpose

To acknowledge receipt of goods or terms of an agreement regarding business transactions or services.

Tone

Simple and direct.

Content Guidelines/Format

1. Describe the goods received or subject of discussion.
2. Specify the date of receipt, order numbers, and other relevant details.
3. Note the date and method of payment (if applicable) or request the recipient's countersignature regarding the agreement.
4. Close with "Cordially."

Helpful Words

able	approve	happy	welcome
accept	glad	pleased	willing

Example

February 5, 20—

Dear Mr. Lobisbo:

Enclosed is a Letter of Agreement between Kane Films and Lobisbo Productions, which outlines the details and terms of the training you will provide to our staff on May 2. Please review the document carefully and then sign and return it to me.

Note that, as requested, I will arrange for a continental breakfast to be set up outside the training facility.

Regards,

Accepting a Proposal

Purpose

To acknowledge acceptance of a proposal.

Tone

Direct.

Content Guidelines/Format

1. State acceptance of proposal. Include title.

2. Emphasize key elements of the proposal (costs, personnel, goals, equipment, materials, responsibilities, liabilities, beginning and completion dates).

3. Close with "Cordially."

Helpful Words

accept	enthusiastic	happy	pleased
advise	excited	inform	
delighted	glad	notify	

Example

June 24, 20—

Dear Ms. Everett:

You will be pleased to learn that we have accepted your self-help article, "How to Like Yourself," for publication in our summer issue. Our editorial board believes the article offers excellent advice for improving self-esteem.

Enclosed for your review is a tentative copy of our standard contract and guidelines prepared by our production director, Joseph Style. Please call me so we can further discuss the contract and guidelines.

Cordially,

Cover Letter for Attached/Enclosed Document

Purpose

To direct the reader's attention to an attached/enclosed document.

Tone

Simple and direct.

Content Guidelines/Format

1. Direct the reader's attention to the additional document.
2. Note the importance or purpose of the attachment or enclosure.
3. If helpful to the reader, summarize key features.
4. If necessary, request that your reader respond to attachment or enclosure.
5. Close with "Cordially."

Helpful Words

attached	features	outline	prospectus
enclosed	included	policy	statement
details	information	procedure	terms

Example

November 25, 20—

Dear Ms. Ruiz:

As requested in your letter of November 21, enclosed is a copy of our annual report for your review. We very much appreciate your interest in our company and hope you find this information useful.

Sincerely,

Billing Adjustment

Purpose

To submit a formal claim for incorrect billing or adjustment of charges.

Tone

Firm but tactful.

Content Guidelines/Format

1. Refer to the incorrect bill or statement's date and number.
2. Explain in detail the reasons for disputing the bill.
3. Specify the correct or adjusted amount due.
4. Request immediate action or adjustment.

Helpful Words

adjust	exchange	rectify	replace
arrange	fix	refund	return
correct	modify	reimburse	
credit	rebate	repair	

Example

September 21, 20—

Dear Mr. Johnson:

On Labor Day weekend, my husband and I took advantage of your holiday sale and purchased an Oriental rug that was discounted from $3,750 to $2,250. We are very happy with the rug. However, when we received our latest bill, the full price of the rug is listed. Obviously this is the result of a billing error, because our receipt lists the discounted price. As my husband and I have been customers of yours for more than 20 years, we are confident you will correct this billing error upon receipt of this letter. I am enclosing a copy of the original receipt and sincerely appreciate your help in this serious matter.

Sincerely,

Claim Adjustment for Merchandise or Services

Purpose

To seek compensation or replacement for a product or service that has failed to function properly or has proven inadequate.

Tone

Firm but tactful.

Content Guidelines/Format

1. Identify the product or service providing all details (product and date of purchase or performance of service). Include serial, product, or model identification numbers.
2. Describe the problem in brief but specific detail.
3. Request adjustment, replacement, or refund.
4. Close with the need for your reader to respond upon receipt of your letter.

Helpful Words

adjust	rectify	reimburse	satisfy
correct	redress	repair	solve
credit	refund	replace	

Example

August 18, 20—

Dear Ms. Consuelo:

Last week when I visited your antique jewelry shop in San Diego, I bought what I believed was a cigarette case from the 1930s, at least that was how it was described on the sales label. When I mentioned to you that I was excited to give the case to my boyfriend because he collected them, you verified that it was indeed a period piece. However, when I returned to Atlanta and gave him the case, he said it was beautiful but on closer examination said it was made in the late 1960s. You can imagine how disappointed I was and am. Perhaps it was an error on your part. Nevertheless, I am returning the case via overnight delivery and expect a refund just as fast.

Sincerely,

Application for Employment

Purpose

To obtain a position or job interview and to highlight key features of a resume.

Tone

Enthusiastic, cordial, and professional.

Content Guidelines/Format

1. State the position for which you are applying.
2. State how your experience and job skills will benefit your potential employer.
3. Stress your desire for a challenging position that fully utilizes all your skills and need for professional growth.
4. Request an interview at the reader's earliest convenience.
5. Close with "Sincerely."

Helpful Words

ability	designed	managed	skill
application	developed	operated	supervised
apply	devised	organized	trained
capable	directed	oversaw	
challenging	experience	planned	
created	initiated	responsible	

Example

April 10, 20—

Dear Mrs. Greene:

I am interested in applying for the Director of Nursing position advertised in yesterday's *Herald*. I have been a nurse since 1975, when I began my nursing career working with Native Americans in the Southwest. I later became an

RN and continued to work at the Medical Center with patients who were economically and socially disadvantaged. In 1990, I moved to New York, where I devoted myself to continuing my educational process. I attended NYU graduate school, worked as part of a prominent research team at their medical center, and ultimately earned my Master's degree. I contributed to the writing of three articles published in *Nursing* magazine. During the years I was in graduate school I shifted my nursing attention to another vulnerable population: the elderly. In the years since and until the present, my responsibilities have included serving as a director of nursing at a nursing home and functioning as a clinical nurse-specialist in an acute-care senior mental health unit.

Two years ago I received a Ph.D. in geriatric nursing. It was not until my current position as Clinical Director for the West Side Home Care Service Group that I worked in the field. There is something very poignant about working with people in their own homes. With respect to the position I am seeking, I can be a strong patient advocate and ensure that clients receive individualized and appropriate care.

With a background that includes supervision and management, medical record review, staff and community education, policies and procedures writing, and overall demonstrated commitment to the promotion of life for all individuals, I believe that as Director of Nursing I can contribute to your organization a positive and effective manner.

Sincerely,

Interview Follow-Up

Purpose

To express appreciation for a job interview.

Tone

Sincere and cordial.

Content Guidelines/Format

1. State appreciation for the interview and your pleasure in meeting the interviewer.
2. Highlight positive aspects of the interview, such as what you may have learned about the job or company.
3. Specify how the interview has added to your enthusiasm for the position and confidence in being able to contribute significantly to the company.
4. Close with your looking forward to hearing from the interviewer.

Helpful Words

appreciate	generous	impressive	thoughtful
assistance	gracious	interesting	unique
enjoyed	grateful	kindness	valuable
fascinating	hospitable	thank you	welcome

Example

August 28, 20—

Dear Mrs. Greene:

I want to express my appreciation for inviting me to interview for the position of Director of Nursing. You very clearly outlined the responsibilities this position entails and offered helpful insights into its demanding nature. I especially am grateful for your taking the time to walk me through the various units at your facility and to introduce me to members of your current supervisory nursing staff. Again, many thanks for your time and most gracious welcome.

Sincerely,

Response to a Complaint

Purpose

To respond to a complaint regarding a product or service.

Tone

Respectful and empathetic.

Content/Format

1. Open with an acknowledgment of the customer's complaint.
2. Respond specifically to the details or circumstances surrounding the complaint.
3. Offer an apology, tangible form of compensation, refund, or willingness to correct the problem.
4. Close cordially with an offer to further assist the customer.

Helpful Words

apologize	inadequate	insufficient	repair
careless	inadvertent	irresponsible	restore
compensate	inconsiderate	misinformed	tactless
deplorable	inconvenient	misleading	thoughtless
disrespectful	incorrect	mistake	unfortunate
failure	ineffective	misunderstanding	unsatisfactory
faulty	inexact	negligible	
flawed	inexcusable	regrettable	
inaccurate	inferior	reimburse	

Example

August 2, 20—

Dear Ms. Marsha:

I want to express my sincere apologies to you for the frustration and anger you experienced last Friday evening at one of our restaurants, House of George and Sam. The server obviously assumed that the item you requested was no longer available at the pre-theater price. I spoke with the manager and he concurred that her actions were inappropriate.

I am very sorry that your birthday celebration was tarnished by the inexcusable service you encountered.

Although no amount of apology can compensate for the unfortunate service you received, please accept the enclosed gift certificate for a complimentary dinner for two at any of our restaurants. I do hope you will allow us another opportunity to serve you.

Cordially,

Response to a Request

Purpose

To respond to a request for information or assistance.

Tone

Cordial.

Content/Format

1. Refer to the date and nature of the request.
2. State what you have done or will do regarding the request.
3. If you're unable to respond, offer an apology and reasons.
4. Close with the hope the reader will be satisfied with your response.

Helpful Words

aid	expedite	hope	request
assistance	glad	immediate	response
expect	happy	pleased	useful

Example

November 25, 20—

Dear Ms. Ramone:

As requested in your letter of November 21, enclosed is a copy of our latest catalogue for your review. We very much appreciate your interest in our company and hope you find this information useful to your needs.

Sincerely,

Negative Response/Refusal

Purpose

To respond negatively to a request, provide bad news, or refuse outright a request for information or assistance.

Tone

Polite and direct.

Content/Format

1. In the opening sentence, express appreciation or a general neutral statement regarding the subject of your correspondence.
2. Present your negative message, followed by reasons, facts, and other supporting data.
3. Close cordially and, if possible, with an offer of future positive action.
4. NOTE: Sensitivity and diplomatic tactfulness are the key ingredients to saying "no" gracefully and with decorum.

Helpful Words

forbid	inhibit	policy	restrict
inability	official	prevent	unable

Example

July 15, 20—

Dear Mr. Malinko:

Mr. Fletcher Hanson has asked me to respond to your letter of July 5, in which you offered the unique services of your company, Escorts on Last Minute Request, to our company.

At this time, there appears to be little need in our company for the delightful services you offer. However, should the need arise among employees or our clients for a last-minute escort we will be certain to contact you. We have entered information about your services into our database for future reference.

Sincerely,

B

Guidelines to Punctuation

Comma

Use a comma in the following instances:

1. To separate items in a series.
   Martha enjoys hiking, swimming, bird-watching, and gardening.

2. After long introductory phrases and clauses often beginning with when, while, if, since, due to, because, although, through, or before.
   When David traveled to Paris, he visited many museums and historic places.

   NOTE: It is often unnecessary to place a comma before or following the words listed here when they occur within a sentence.
   David visited many museums and historic places when he traveled to Paris.

3. To set off parenthetical or interruptive words and phrases.
   Janet, who is a lawyer, has moved to Arizona.

4. To indicate a pause.
   Last summer I read many books about gardening, all of which were excellent.

5. Before a conjunction (and, but, or, nor, so, for, yet) that connects two independent sentences.

Susan is a highly accomplished musician, and her brother is a successful screenwriter.

6. After "yes" and "no" if they begin a sentence.
   Yes, our company has been awarded the contract.

7. After words of address.
   Joe, that was an excellent presentation.

8. To set off dates and places.
   August 19, 2002
   Atlanta, Georgia

9. To introduce quotations.
   In Joseph Mature's opinion, "Staff training is essential to our corporate growth."

10. To set off titles and degrees.
    Evan Douglas, M.A.
    Gianna Lucia, Director of Publicity, will speak at the conference today.

When Not to Use a Comma

Do *not* use a comma in the following instances:

1. To connect two independent sentences without inserting a connecting conjunction (*and, or, but, for, nor, so, yet*).
   The company is moving to Florida, Jack has decided to remain in New York.

2. After subordinating conjunctions (*when, while, after, if, since, because, before, although, after*) either in the beginning or middle of a sentence.
   Although, she wanted to attend the conference, Carol was too busy to take time off.
   I bought a new computer because, my old one was outdated.

3. Instead of a semicolon (*however, nevertheless, moreover, subsequently, next, therefore, finally, in conclusion, consequently, as a result, on the contrary, on the other hand, also, furthermore*) to connect two independent sentences.
   George did an excellent job on the project, as a result, he received a bonus.

Semicolon

Use a semicolon in the following instances:

1. To join two independent sentences that bear a relationship such as cause/effect, problem/solution, comparison/contrast, or time/time.
   This book is extremely rare; it is very valuable.

2. To join two independent sentences connected by *however, nevertheless, for example, on the other hand, on the contrary, subsequently, this, first, next, last, in conclusion, finally, moreover, accordingly, otherwise, still, furthermore, also,* or *then.*
   My girlfriend has been promoted to Director of Nursing; moreover, she has just published her first book.

3. To separate items in a series that contains internal commas.
   The following individuals have been appointed to our board of directors: Leonard Stile, Vice President for Public Affairs, Arista Bank; Alan Gordon, Chairman, Zizka Corporation; Joseph Gandi, Senior Partner, Gandi Technology & Software Ltd.

Colon

Use a colon when you want to:

1. Introduce a list or series.
   The following goals have been accomplished:

2. Indicate emphasis.
   These are the qualities of effective writing: clarity and precision.

Parentheses

Use parentheses in the following instance:

1. To enclose information provided to clarify or explain information.

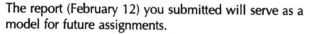
The report (February 12) you submitted will serve as a model for future assignments.

2. *Do not* confuse parentheses with brackets. Brackets are used to indicate a writer's changes or additions to quoted material.

   Larry stated: "[Paul] Nelson's report last month [July] is the best I've seen in years."

Question Mark

Use a question mark to distinguish a direct question from one that is paraphrased.

- **Direct:** Carlo asked his wife, What time are you leaving for Vermont?

- **Indirect:** Carlo asked his wife when she was leaving for Vermont.

Em-Dash

Use the dash selectively to substitute for a comma, semicolon, parentheses, or colon.

   All the players—including the coach—attended the celebration party.

Apostrophe

The apostrophe is used in the following ways:

1. To indicate possession by a single noun (add an "s" following the apostrophe).
   Mel's art collection
   the firm's new offices

2. To indicate possession by a plural noun (do not add an "s" following the apostrophe).
   the girls' coats

3. To indicate possession by a name or word ending in "s" or "z."
   Doris's house

4. To form contractions.
   - I'll   (I will)
   - hasn't (has not)
   - they'd (they would)
   - it's   (it is)
   - Do not use an apostrophe to indicate possession by the pronoun "it" (its).
     The dog wagged its tail.

5. To form the plural of numbers and letters.
   A's
   7's

   Note: Do not place an apostrophe before an "s" when denoting a plural acronym.
   SOPs

Hyphen

Use a hyphen in the following instances:

1. Two or more words used to describe or modify a single noun.
   first-rate report
   on-the-job training

2. With compound numbers (21–99).
   twenty-five
   one hundred and fifty-seven

3. With prefixes.
   ex-president
   pro-American
   mid-August

4. To separate words to avoid confusion.
   The wood must be re-treated with the varnish after one hour.

   Note: These are basic simple rules for using the hyphen. Because there are many compound words that either are written as solid words (*longtime*) or separate with no hyphenation (*data processing*), it is always wise to consult a dictionary to avoid mistakes.

C

Grammar and Usage Review

Subject and Verb Agreement

A subject and verb must agree in number and person.

	Singular	**Plural**
First person:	I walk	we walk
Second person:	you walk	you walk
Third person:	he walks	
	she walks	they walk
	it walks	

Most writers have little problem with typical sentences that have either a clearly singular or plural subject, such as the following sentences:

The Brooklyn Bridge **connects** Brooklyn with Manhattan.
Martha writes and **edits** medical reports.
The cars **are parked** across the street.

Collective Nouns

Collective nouns refer to a group of people or objects. They take singular form verbs when indicating a single group or unit. For example:

assembly	board	commission	council
association	cabinet	committee	crowd
audience	class	company	department

faculty	group	majority	orchestra
family	information	management	public
firm	jury	minority	staff

The committee **is** meeting today.

Note: Plural collective nouns take plural verb forms.

The committees **are** meeting today.

🖊 🖊 🖊

The following collective nouns are singular although they appear plural in form:

news

apparatus

series

summons

The World Series **is** always exciting.

On the other hand, these collective nouns are plural:

| assets | odds | profits | wages |
| earnings | premises | savings | winnings |

Indefinite Pronouns

Indefinite pronouns do not refer to anyone or anything in particular and require singular verbs.

Everyone **is** waiting to meet you.

Here is a list of indefinite pronouns:

anybody	anything	every	everything
anyone	each	everyone	neither
any one	either	everybody	

When two singular words are joined by *or, either...or, neither...nor*, the verb is singular:

Either William or Mary **is** going to receive the award.

When two plural words are joined by *or, either...or, neither...nor*, the verb is plural:

Neither the students nor their parents **are** pleased with the news of a tuition increase.

When a singular and plural words are joined by *or, either...or, neither...nor*, the verb agrees with the word closer to it:

Either the manager or her assistants **are** going to edit the report.

Words That Measure

Words that denote measurement often require a singular verb:

Fifty dollars **is** the average price of dinner in the new restaurant.

However, when the items being measured are viewed individually, use a plural verb:

Fifty dollars (bills) **are** in the jar.

When fractions and expressions that denote measurement are followed by a prepositional phrase beginning with *of*, the object of the phrase determines if the verb is singular or plural:

One-half of the report **has** been completed.

One-half of the reports **have** been completed.

The term *the number* is singular, but *a number* is plural:

The number of cardinals I've seen this spring **is** surprising.

A number of birds **are** gathering on my lawn this morning.

Titles and Names

Individual titles of books, newspapers, magazines, journals, reports, manuals, plays, courses, subjects, and names of companies and organizations are always followed by a singular verb.

The *New York Times* **is** a famous newspaper.

Physics **is** a difficult subject for many people.

Romeo and Juliet **is** one of Shakespeare's most popular plays.

Verb Forms

Some verbs can be troublesome because they change their forms depending on the tense. Some words are always the same, such as *cut, bid, burst, read,* and *set*. Remember that with few exceptions the irregular verbs listed here change their spelling to form the past tense:

Present Tense	Past Tense	Past Participle*
arise	arose	arisen
awake	awoke	awoken
be (am, is, are)	was, were	been
begin	began	begun
bite	bit	bitten
blow	blew	blown
break	broke	broken
buy	bought	bought
catch	caught	caught
choose	chose	chosen
come	came	come
creep	crept	crept
dive	dove	dove
do	did	done
drag	dragged	dragged
dream	dreamed, dreamt	dreamt
draw	drew	drawn
dwell	dwelt	dwelt
drink	drank	drunk
drive	drove	driven
eat	ate	eaten
fall	fell	fallen
flee	fled	fled
fling	flung	flung
fly	flew	flown
forget	forgot	forgotten

Present Tense	Past Tense	Past Participle*
freeze	froze	frozen
get	got	gotten
go	went	gone
grow	grew	grown
hide	hid	hidden
know	knew	known
lay (to place)	laid	laid
lie (to recline)	lay	lain
lie (to falsify)	lied	lied
light	lit	lit
lose	lost	lost
mean	meant	meant
meet	met	met
pay	paid	paid
prove	proved	proven
ride	rode	ridden
ring	rang	rung
rise	rose	risen
run	ran	run
say	said	said
see	saw	seen
seek	sought	sought
shake	shook	shaken
shine (to beam)	shone	shone
shine (to polish)	shined	shined
show	showed	shown
sing	sang	sung
sink	sank	sunk
sit	sat	sat
slide	slid	slid
speak	spoke	spoken
spring	sprang	sprung
steal	stole	stolen
sting	stung	stung

Present Tense	Past Tense	Past Participle*
strive	strove	striven
swear	swore	sworn
swim	swam	swum
swing	swung	swung
take	took	taken
teach	taught	taught
tear	tore	torn
tell	told	told
throw	threw	thrown
wear	wore	worn
weave	wove	woven
write	wrote	written

*Note: Past participle verbs denote (1) an action or activity that started in the past and is ongoing or continuing or (2) a more recent or immediate past action or activity. These verb forms are always preceded by *am, was, were, has, has been, have, have been, had,* or *had been.*

Examples

John has written manuals for our company for 20 years. (ongoing activity)

The boy has broken the window. (recent action)

Pronoun Agreement

Personal pronouns in various forms are listed here:

	Subject	Object	Possessive
First Person:	I, we	me, us	my, our
Second Person:	you	you	your
Third Person:	he	him	his
	she	her	her
	it	it	its
	they	them	their

Personal Pronouns

A personal pronoun, whether singular or plural, must always agree with its antecedent (the word to which the pronoun refers). For example:

Pamela is very happy with her new haircut.

The students were anxious to take their final exams.

Indefinite Pronouns

Indefinite pronouns do not refer to anyone or anything in particular. They include the following:

any	either	neither	someone
anyone	every	no one	
each	everyone	some	

When they are singular, both the verb any personal pronouns that follow in the same sentence will be singular. For example:

Each of the ballplayers has signed a five-year contract.

Anyone who was there that evening will always remember the fun he or she had.

Every manager is planning to attend the presentation skills workshop.

Note: When using the phrase *either...or* and *neither...nor* use the noun closest to the verb to determine if the verb form is singular or plural. For example:

Either Jeremy or Francisco is going to win the prize.

Neither the managers nor their assistants are working late this week.

Neither the president or nor his representatives have decided to attend the conference.

Either his representatives or the president is planning to attend the conference.

Comparative and Sentence-Completion Pronouns

Sentences that contain comparative references or incomplete clauses often use a subject rather than object pronoun. For example:

Tony has more experience than I. (than I have)
Alexis and Mark play tennis better than we. (than we play)

Pronouns Following Prepositions

Use object pronouns following prepositions. For example:

Between you and me, this is a great investment.
Sam gave the assignment to Grace and me.

Often-Confused Words

Here is a list of words confused in meaning and where one letter can make all the difference between praise and damnation. All are certain to baffle your spell-checker:

accept - to receive favorably
except - to leave out

ad - an advertisement
add - to increase

adapt - to adjust
adept - skilled
adopt - to take for one's own

addition - something added
edition - the number or manner of a published work

adverse - opposing, unfavorable
averse to - disinclined towards, reluctant

advice - a recommendation
advise - to counsel

agenda - a list of tasks or goals
addenda - additional

affect - to influence
effect (noun) - a result
effect (verb) - to bring about, to accomplish

aid - to help
aide - an assistant

allusion - a reference
illusion - a visual deception
delusion - a false notion or idea

aloud - audible
allowed - permitted

already - previously
all ready - in readiness

alternate - a substitute
alternative - a choice between two

altogether - entirely
all together - as one group, united
all right - standard English spelling

ante - before
anti - against

anyway - in any event
any way - in any way or manner

appraise - to estimate the value of
apprize - to inform

assent - to consent
ascent - a rise

assistance - help
assistants - helpers

beside - next to
besides - moreover, in addition

better - of higher quality
bettor - one who gambles

blue - a color
blew - past tense of the verb "blow"

bolder - fearless, daring
boulder - a large rock

brake - to stop from moving
break - to fracture, interrupt

born - brought into life
borne - carried, endured

capital - chief, important
capitol - a building or site of official city or seat of government

casual - informal
causal - the source or cause

cite - to summon or quote
site - a location
sight - vision

coarse - unrefined
course - a passage, route, subject of study

confidant - one to whom secrets are entrusted
confident - possessed of self-assurance

contemptible - deserving contempt
contemptuous - expressing contempt

continuation - pertains to length or sequence
continual - pertains to time, interrupted occurrences
continuous - occurs without interruption

council - an assembly of individuals whose purpose is to advise, govern, or legislate
counsel - an advisor, an attorney

credible - believable
credulous - prone to belief
creditable - deserving esteem, praise-worthy

dear - valued, loved
deer - an animal

decent - respectable, proper
descent - a downward movement
dissent - disagreement

decree - a decision or ruling
degree - a step or point in a series, acknowledgment of academic accomplishment

definite - clear
definitive - final, official

deprecate - to express disapproval of
depreciate - to decrease in value
desecrate - to treat irreverently

device - a contrivance, object
devise - to contrive, create, invent

disburse - to pay out
disperse - to scatter

disinterested - impartial
uninterested - not interested

disprove - to prove false
disapprove - to not approve

exalt - to praise
exult - to rejoice

eligible - qualified
legible - plain, easy to read

envelop - to surround
envelope - stationery

exceed - to surpass, go beyond
accede - to yield, surrender

except - to leave out, exclude
accept - to receive with approval

expand - to increase
expend - to spend

extant - existing
extinct - non-existing
extent - the measure, length, degree

facetious - causing laughter
fictitious - unreal

fare - a price
fair - impartial

farther - pertains to distance
further - additional

feat - an accomplishment
feet - plural form of "foot"

fewer - refers to countable things
less - refers to uncountable

flair - natural style, ability, talent
flare - a glowing light used to indicate location or warning

formerly - previously
formally - dignified, seriously

fortunate - lucky
fortuitous - happening by chance

genius - inspired ability, talent, skill
genus - classification of a species

homogenous - of common origin
homogeneous - composed of similar elements or parts

human - pertaining to mankind
humane - compassionate, merciful

hypercritical - overly critical
hypocritical - deceitful

illegible - unable to be read
illegal - unlawful

illicit - unlawful
elicit - to draw out

imply - to suggest indirectly
infer - to deduce or conclude

immoral - not moral
immortal - cannot die

incredible - unbelievable
incredulous - unbelieving

inept - awkward, foolish
inapt - unqualified, unsuited

inequity - not equal, unfair
iniquity - evil

insight - understanding of, knowledge of
incite - to arouse to action

insure - to guarantee against financial loss
ensure - to make sure or certain

intelligent - possessed of intelligence
intelligible - understandable, comprehensible

its - possessive form of the pronoun "it"
it's - contraction form of "it is" or "it has"

lay - to place, set down
lie - to recline

lend - verb for temporary use
loan - noun for temporary use

lesson - instruction
lessen - to reduce

liable - responsible, likely to
libel - written, published, spoken defamation of character

moral - pertaining to right conduct
morale - state of mind, feeling, or spirit

pare - to trim, scale down
pair - two of a kind
pear - a fruit

perpetrate - to carry out, to be guilty of
perpetuate - to make lasting

personal - individual, private
personnel - employees, workers, members of an organization

precede - to go before or ahead
proceed - to advance

precedence - priority
precedents - established rules or procedures

preview - to view in advance
purview - range, scope, limits of

principal - chief, main
principle - rule

prophesy - to predict
prophecy - prediction

quiet - absent of noise
quite - to an extent

sea - body of water
see - present tense of "to see"

soar - to fly or rise above
sore - painful

sometime - at an indefinite time
some time - a period of time
sometimes - now and then, on occasion

stationary - permanent, unmovable
stationery - writing paper and associated supplies

tantamount - equivalent
paramount - the highest

taught - instructed
taut - tense, tightly wound

temerity - boldness
timidity - shyness, fearful

than - comparison
then - time, following

their - possessive pronoun
there - indicates location or reference
they're - contraction form of "they are"

through - from beginning to end
thorough - completely, fully

threw - past tense of verb "to throw"
thru - nonstandard spelling of "through"

to - a preposition
too - also, much
two - a number

typical - conforming to type or expectation
atypical - nonconforming to type, irregular

unabridged - entire, complete
abridged - shortened version
expurgated - objectionable content removed

unreal - not real
unreel - to unwind

use - present tense verb
used - past tense verb

vary - to change
very - much

veracious - truthful
voracious - greedy, hungry

vice - moral fault
vise - tool

waver - to fluctuate
waiver - to suspend or relinquish

weak - not strong
week - seven days

whose - possessive pronoun
who's - contraction form of "who is" or "who has"

your - possessive pronoun
you're - contraction form of "you are"
yore - of times past

Correct Use of Prepositions That Follow Certain Words

accompanied

by	a person
with	a thing

account

for	an action
to	a person

adapt

from	patterned after
to	adjusted or modified for

agree

in	to be like, similar
on	to be in accord with
to	to consent
with	to concur

angry

with	a person
about	a situation

capacity

for	ability

of   content or space

compare

to   to express similarities
with   to express differences

confer

about   to discuss
upon   to bestow or grant

correspond

to   agree with
with   communicate through writing

differ

from   to be different
in   disagreement regarding an issue
with   disagree with a person

different

from

disappointed

by, in   someone
with   something

speak, talk

with   a person
to   address a group or an audience

 F

Capitalization

Here are the basic rules for capitalization:

Capitalize the names of persons, places, and things that have a proper meaning:

Joseph Raggio
Blue Ridge
Stratford Green Lane
London
Oxford University

Do not capitalize common nouns that denote a general meaning:

nurse
street
college
company

Capitalize the proper names of organizations:

United Nations
California State Highway Commission
Department of the Treasury

Capitalize the names of countries, states, specific geographic regions, holidays, days of the week, months, and historic events:

Italy
Wisconsin
the Southeast
Christmas
Thursday

August
the War of 1812

NOTE: Do not capitalize the seasons (winter, spring, summer, fall).

Capitalize titles following names:

Joseph Neil, Director of Market Research
Alan Vanucci, Vice President for Public Affairs

Capitalize key words in titles of publications:

The *New York Times*
People
Ladies Home Journal

Plural Nouns

The plural of the majority of nouns is formed by adding an "s" at the end.

car	cars
desk	desks
pen	pens
song	song
nurse	nurses

The plural of nouns ending in a "y" preceded by a vowel (a, e, i, o, u) is formed by adding an "s."

play	plays
toy	toys
attorney	attorneys
decoy	decoys
journey	journeys

The plural of nouns ending in a "y" preceded by a consonant is formed by changing the "y" to an "i" and adding "es."

study	studies
lady	ladies
sky	skies
enemy	enemies
treaty	treaties

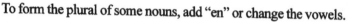

To form the plural of some nouns, add "en" or change the vowels.

child	children
man	men
woman	women
tooth	teeth
mouse	mice

To form the plural of nouns ending in "ch," "s," "sh," "x," or "z," add "es" to the end.

lunch	lunches
bus	buses
brush	brushes
box	boxes
waltz	waltzes

The plural of some nouns ending in "f" and "fe" is formed by changing the "f" to "ve" or adding an "s."

leaf	leaves
half	halves
wife	wives
wolf	wolves
proof	proofs
belief	beliefs
roof	roofs
cafe	cafes

The plural of many nouns ending in "o" is formed by adding an "s" to the ending.

piano	pianos
casino	casinos
radio	radios
soprano	sopranos

The plural of some nouns ending in "o" is formed by adding an "es" to the ending.

hero	heroes
potato	potatoes
tomato	tomatoes
veto	vetoes

Some hyphenated words only form the plural of the key word.

brother-in-law	brothers-in-law
attorney-at-law	attorneys-at-law
hanger-on	hangers-on
maid-of-honor	maids-of-honor

Some words ending in "s" take singular verbs.

mathematics
physics
politics
economics
news

When used as nouns, some words are only plural.

proceeds
tweezers
scissors
trousers
clothes
thanks
pants
billiards
belongings

Some words indicate both plural and singular.

deer
fish
moose
salmon
sheep
trout

Compound Nouns/Words

Compound nouns consist of two or more words hyphenated or written as solid or separate words. Some familiar compound words are *brother-in-law, checklist,* and *data processing.* Although your spell-checker will often prove helpful when using compound words, if in doubt, always consult an up-to-date dictionary for the correct spelling. Here is a selected list of compound words:

age-old	bylaw	crossroad
accident-prone	capital-intensive	custom-made
airmail	carsick	cutoff
attorney-at-law	cave-in	data processing
audiovisual	changeover	daylong
backup	check-in	double-spaced
bankroll	checklist	drawback
biweekly	checkup	drive-in
blackout	cleanup	eye-catching
book review	closeout	eye-opener
bookstore	coauthor	eyewitness
brainstorm	comeback	fireproof
breakaway	computer-aided	follow-through
breakdown	cost-effective	follow-up
breakout	countdown	full-bodied
breakthrough	courtyard	get-together
breakup	crackdown	good-bye
broad-minded	cross-reference	good-natured
buildup	cross section	goodwill

habit-forming
hair-raising
half hour
half-truth
handbook
heartsick
high-priced
homesick
hometown
interest-bearing
interoffice
know-how
law-abiding
lifelong
lifestyle
life raft
long-winded
market-tested
masterpiece
master plan
middle-aged
misspell

moneymaker
money order
multipurpose
nationwide
nightlife
nonessential
old-fashioned
panic-stricken
paperwork
praiseworthy
proactive
quick-tempered
quick-witted
reorganize
retroactive
runaway
run-through
salespeople
schoolteacher
semiannual
send-off
show-off

sky-high
spin-off
standby
subdivision
takeoff
takeover
tax-exempt
tax-sheltered
time-saver
time sheet
top-heavy
trade name
trustworthy
trade-off
tryout
turnover
user-friendly
walk-through
weatherproof
workout
write-off
year-round

Writing Aerobics

Review Exercises
to Test Yourself

1.

Use familiar or simpler words to express the following ideas.

accomplish the project   —————————

effectuate improvement   —————————

render every assistance   —————————

enclosed herewith please find   —————————

pursuant to   —————————

make reference to   —————————

perform an examination   —————————

close proximity   —————————

ameliorate   —————————

anterior to   —————————

append   —————————

adjacent to   —————————

approbation   —————————

elucidate   —————————

peruse   —————————

thereupon   —————————

2.

Revise the following sentences for greater precision and economy of expression.

1. In accordance with your request, distribution of the questionnaires has been accomplished.
2. This technique serves the function of being of use for processing orders without delay.
3. This is to inform you that per request of yours to ordering new computer equipment we will proceed to do so within seven days.
4. Victor Young was asked to conduct a study of the progress of several of the reports being written by managers proposing revising various internal procedures.
5. Tina needs to make a decision with respect as to whether or not she will apply for a management position with another company.
6. The software was designed in order to effectuate improvement of accounting procedures and practices.
7. Pursuant to questions concerning revised guidelines for writing policies, a meeting is scheduled for May 27 to ensure clarification of the above-mentioned guidelines.

3.

Revise the following memo.

TO: Department Supervisors
FROM: Sam Gold
SUBJECT: Departmental Relocation Plan

As you all know, our new building will be ready for occupancy in the fall. I have therefore been working with our Corporate Structure Department on plans to combine and relocate various departments now occupying our current building. These moves will relocate all departments to our new location Blue Ridge Street. Procurement and Purchasing will be the first departments to be relocated, followed by Accounting, Engineering, and Human Resources. For your convenience I have attached herewith a detailed plan showing the exact location of each of your departments so you can provide urgently needed suggestions and requests for furniture and other necessary equipment requirements. I need these comments by next Friday.

4.

Proofread and correct the following message.

Emergency calls from George,

George called Dave and I last Tuesday @ 10;30 am George's personal e-mail is not working in the Internet ABC. So I contracted John and her assistant to inform him that I could not make it to the meeting, because I have an emergency meeting with George. I install the ABC but the Internet male was still not working. I received the messaging One or more applications have been use by other applications Please close all the applications and start the ABC again. I closed all the applications but still have a problem. I called Tom, he suggested to downlow the ABC so I did this: but its still not working. I called tom again and spoke to a different support person. He said install the ABC again I did and I tested the connection and E-mail with no problem. I finally got the E-mail to work again for George.

5.

Revise the following memo for economy and tone.

TO: All staff
FROM: G. Regrotty
SUBJECT: Personal Use of Office Copiers

This week a very serious problem was brought to my attention by a dedicated employee. The problem involves personnel making excessive use of office copiers for their own private purposes. Official company policy states clearly and emphatically that office copiers are to be used exclusively for official business only. Nevertheless as in any organization there are those individuals who prefer to ignore company policy and act contrary to official procedures.

Those guilty of this must at once cease and desist said activities and the abuse of official policy. I wish to make myself perfectly clear in this matter that continued refutation of established procedures will not be tolerated and will result in immediate dismissal. Please feel free to forward comments and questions regarding this issue to my direct attention. Thank you.

Answers to Writing Aerobics

1.

accomplish the project	COMPLETE THE PROJECT
effectuate improvement	IMPROVE
render every assistance	HELP, ASSIST
enclosed herewith please find	ENCLOSED
pursuant to	REGARDING, ACCORDING TO
make reference to	REFER
perform an examination	EXAMINE
close proximity	NEAR
ameliorate	IMPROVE
anterior to	BEFORE
append to	ADD
approbation	APPROVAL
elucidate	DEFINE, EXPLAIN
peruse	VIEW
thereupon	THEN

2.

1. As requested, the questionnaires have been distributed.
2. This technique can process orders without delay.
3. As you requested, we will order the new computer equipment within seven days.

4. Victor Young was asked to study the progress of managers' internal procedures reports.

5. Tina needs to decide if she will apply for a management position with another company.

6. The software was designed to improve accounting procedures.

7. We have scheduled a meeting for May 27 to clarify questions about the guidelines for writing policies.

3.

TO: Department Supervisors
FROM: Sam Gold
SUBJECT: Departmental Relocation Plan

Please review the enclosed department relocation plan and return all requests for furniture and equipment requirements to me no later than Friday, July 10.

4.

Emergency call from George

George called Dave and **me** last Tuesday **at** 10:30 am. George's personal e-mail **was** not working in the Internet ABC. So I **contacted** John and **his** assistant to inform **them** that I could not make it to the meeting because I **had** an emergency meeting with George. I **installed** the ABC but the Internet **mail** was still not working. I received the **message** "One or more applications have been **used** by other applications. Please close all the applications and start the ABC again." I closed all the applications but still **had** a problem. I called Tom, **and** he suggested **downloading** the ABC so I did this but **it's** still not working. I called **Tom** again and spoke **with** a different support person. He said to install the ABC again **and I did.** I tested the connection and E-mail with no problem. I finally got the E-mail to work again for George.

5.

TO: All staff
FROM: G. Regrotty
SUBJECT: Personal Use of Office Copiers

Official policy states that office copiers are to be used only for official business. Nevertheless, I have learned that employees have been making use of copiers for private use. Unofficial use of copiers is costly and time-consuming.

At the same time, I realize the occasional need for personal copies and so have directed G. Lawrence to make the copier in room 2C available for personal use either lunch hours or before or after work. Please remember to enter your name and number of copies on the sign-in sheet. Because there will be no charge for this privilege, I expect no employees will abuse it.

Index

About the Author

Salvatore J. Iacone, Ph.D., is a management training consultant specializing in designing and conducting highly successful business and technical writing workshops for corporations, government agencies, and universities. Clients have included AT&T, Georgia-Pacific, Duracell, Pfizer, Maher Terminals, Honeywell, and IBM, among others. Dr. Iacone is the author of several books and articles and holds a Ph.D. from St. John's University. Information about his seminars can be obtained by contacting his Website: *siwriting.com* or *siacone@aol.com.*